REVISED EDITION

SO-BDR-742

Management
Me$_s$s-Ups

57 Pitfalls You Can Avoid
(And Stories of Those Who Didn't)

MARK EPPLER

CAREER
PRESS

Franklin Lakes, N.J.

Copyright © 2006 by Mark Eppler

All rights reserved under the Pan-American and International Copyright Conventions. This book may not be reproduced, in whole or in part, in any form or by any means electronic or mechanical, including photocopying, recording, or by any information storage and retrieval system now known or hereafter invented, without written permission from the publisher, The Career Press.

MANAGEMENT MESS-UPS, REVISED EDITION
Cover design by DesignConcept
Printed in the U.S.A. by Book-mart Press

To order this title, please call toll-free 1-800-CAREER-1 (NJ and Canada: 201-848-0310) to order using VISA or MasterCard, or for further information on books from Career Press.

The Career Press, Inc., 3 Tice Road, PO Box 687,
Franklin Lakes, NJ 07417
www.careerpress.com

Library of Congress Cataloging-in-Publication Data

Eppler, Mark, 1946-
    Management mess-ups : 57 pitfalls you can avoid (and stories of those who didn't) / Mark Eppler.— Rev. ed.
        p.cm.
    Includes index.
    ISBN 1-56414-848-3 (paper)
        1. Management. 2. Executives. 3. Organizational effectiveness.
    I. Title.

    HD31.E67 2005
658.4--dc22

                                        2005050777

Acknowledgements

Ben Franklin once wrote that his wisdom was the "collective gleanings" of others. There are so many from whom I have gleaned wisdom that mentioning them all is impossible. A few, however, must be acknowledged, and to them I dedicate this book.

The late Norman Vincent Peale, whose letter of encouragement ("Keep writing, Mark, you'll never know whose life you might touch") was and is an inspiration.

Rick, Chad, Cathy, Dave—and all the other family members and friends whose involvement in my life made this job easier.

To all the editors at Career Press whose professionalism and skill help turn "caterpillars" into "butterflies."

Stephanie and Carrie, two of the best daughters a man could hope to have, who both encouraged and admonished me to get the book done.

Linda, my wife and best friend, who patiently read my manuscript over and over, offering valuable and much-needed insight.

My mother and father who, both individually and jointly, gave me a love for ideas and a vision that I might express them in a format such as this.

Lastly, my late mother-in-law, Lila Bush, who gave me the best review of all: "This is a relationship book. Parents need to read this as well as managers."

Contents

Part 1: Leadership   19

Part 2: Communication   39

Part 6: Problem Solving   121

Part 7: Customer Service   145

Part 8: Getting Results   163

Foreword

When I first wrote *Management Mess-Ups*, my goal was to write a book that would have "staying power." I wanted to write something useful and practical enough that people would buy it and read it, then keep it handy for future reference. I knew it was a modest offering in the annals of management literature, but I wanted it to stand the test of time. I never dreamed that the "test" would be so severe.

In the seven years since this book was first published, the changes in our world have been mind-numbing, with the effect on business and management profound. Consider just three:

- ❖ The specter of terrorism on our own shores has altered everything from homeland security to worker values. Employees, having witnessed the horrors of 9/11, are re-examining what's really important. Many are placing meaningful purpose ahead of money as a key factor in the work they seek.

- ❖ Corporate scandals rocked business and Wall Street at the beginning of the new millennium. It took sweeping legislation (Sarbanes-Oxley) requiring CEOs to personally certify their financials to lure investors back into the marketplace. The impact on workers was an increase in cynicism and a reduction in loyalty.

❖ Technology advances and cost reductions dramatically altered the manner in which we interface with each other. PDAs, laptops, and wireless technology redefined the how, when, and where of business communication. Employees began to feel a sense of detachment as e-mails, seven-trillion annually, replaced more personal forms of communication.

Managers and leaders are dealing with problems they never dreamed of in their forward planning a decade ago. The explosive rise in outsourcing (the person taking your order at McDonald's is in Bangalore), the demand for organic growth, shifting alliances (internal and external), mercurial markets and quixotic customers all have served, in some fashion, to alter the landscape of business.

In my seminars, I refer to this period in time as the Age of Inherent Instability. Some are discomfited by this title because it implies a world full of uncertainty, ambiguity, and change. They look longingly at the past and hope things will return to "normal." This, however, is the New Normal. There's good news, though. The opportunities of this age far outweigh its threats.

The survivors

Business today is relying less on mergers and acquisitions, and is looking instead for growth opportunities within core competencies. The burden of increasing organic growth (the net growth of a company after subtracting all "other factors") has been shifted back to managers at all levels who are charged with becoming true growth leaders. This requires managers (and workers) who understand the difference between tasks and outcomes, and who take ownership of the latter.

Remarkably, *Management Mess-Ups* has indeed stood the test of time. The reasons have less to do with my skill as a writer than they do with the fact that the principles they're based on are solid, and therefore will always be relevant and timely. Will there ever be a point when we no longer need to remind ourselves to be effective listeners? Will connecting with customers to discover their needs ever go out of vogue? Will there come a moment when we no longer need to remember that equity drives everything? Not likely. Truth is truth, even when packaged in the deceptive form of common sense. As Tom Peters notes in *The Circle of Innovation*, it doesn't have to be new to be dramatic.

Introduction

"People who accept correction are on the
pathway to life, but those who ignore it will lead
others astray."

—Proverbs 10:17 (NLT)

Can you imagine losing a $2-million customer over
60 cents? It happened several years ago in Spokane,
Washington. According to a story reported by *USA
Today* ("Bank Gets $2M Lesson"), John Barrier had a
bad bank experience. After cashing a check for $100 at a
branch office, Barrier asked the receptionist to validate his
parking ticket. She refused, noting that he had not executed
a "transaction." Barrier informed the lady he was a substantial depositor, but received a big "so what" look for his
trouble. He appealed to the branch manager, who mechani-
cally recited the bank's policy regarding parking tickets.
The next day, a frustrated John Barrier walked into the main
office and closed out his account—a little over $2 million.

I keep a well-worn copy of this story in my wallet as a
reminder that in business, little errors can have big consequences. I call these errors "Mess-Ups." The real mess-up
in this story was not committed by the receptionist, but by
the bank's management team. Any policy that comes between

a company and its attempt to satisfy customer needs should be subject to immediate revision. (See Mess-Up No. 30 for more on this topic.) Although the previous story may seem like an isolated incident, the reality is that companies are loosing this amount, and more, every day. They're just doing it in smaller, harder-to-track increments.

The problem

Managing in today's turbulent business environment is one tough assignment! When you consider the decentralization of power and authority in today's flatter, downsized organizations, you quickly realize that being held accountable for the productivity and performance of other people is no small responsibility. Add to an already difficult assignment the fact that many of today's managers are ill-prepared for the task, and you have a potent formula for failure.

Companies all over the world, even those of greatest repute, are discovering the high cost of losing good employees. And, as countless exit interviews are revealing, the reasons for the departures are often minor ones. By committing an endless number of small mistakes (mess-ups), managers are driving talented people out the door. The ones remaining aren't too happy either. As one worker told me recently, "You can work for the greatest company in the world, but if you have a bad boss, you have a lousy job."

The remedy

Management Mess-Ups: 57 Pitfalls You Can Avoid (and Stories of Those Who Didn't) offers practical, timely advice for those responsible for getting work done with and through other people. It's concise, humorous, insightful, and highly accessible. The information presented is real-world stuff, gleaned from the comments and experiences of hundreds of seminar participants and clients worldwide. Care has been taken, however, to refer to no companies or individuals by name. We want the principles presented to stand on their own merit.

Learning from the mistakes

The primary purpose of a business is to attract and retain customers. The primary purpose of management is to create a work environment where workers are equipped, empowered, and self-motivated to accomplish this business goal. Creating such a work environment requires managers who possess a variety of conceptual, technical, and human-relations skill. No skill, however, may be as important as the ability to learn and grow from past mistakes—either one's own or those of others.

Part 1:
Leadership

Mess-Up No. 1

Failure to understand that the true objective of a manager is to create stars, not to be one.

"Troubles arise, not over inequalities of property, but over inequalities of honor."

—Aristotle

The purchasing manager of a West Coast company was conducting an on-site audit of Acme Components, a potential new supplier she was concerned about using. If selected, Acme would not only become a "sole source" supplier for her company, but the smallest one they dealt with. In an effort to resolve her concerns, she held a meeting with the staff of Acme and began asking a series of "what if" questions. What if the factory burned down, what if the machines producing the parts crashed, and so on. She was a little surprised that every question was answered by the general manager, despite the fact that his whole staff was present at the meeting.

As the audit drew to a close, she turned and addressed one last question to the man who had dominated the meeting. "What would happen," she asked, "if something happened to you?" The "Mack Truck" question should have been an easy one to respond to. In this case, it was asked because the GM had positioned himself as the key person at Acme. Here was an opportunity not only to alleviate the concerns of the person asking the question, but to champion the capabilities of team members as well.

While everyone, staff as well as potential customers, waited for a reply, the general manager shrugged his shoulders and assumed an expression that seemed to say, "You're quite right, I am the key to this whole operation." Although the words had not actually been uttered, his silence and posture spoke volumes. Instead of allaying the buyer's concern by championing his group, he chose to bask in the warm glow of self-importance. In that self-indulgent moment a large contract was lost. So, perhaps, were the respect and loyalty of his staff.

I remember a similar situation where the same question was asked of another company president. He thought it was amusing. "I only hope," he chuckled, "that someone will notice I'm gone!" He went on to extol the virtues of what he called "the best staff in America." "I trust I would be missed," he concluded, "but this company would continue as before." That's the kind of answer one would expect from a star maker, a manager who champions the efforts of his team. It's a shame the general manager at Acme didn't respond in a similar fashion. He, too, was surrounded by a capable staff—a staff more than able to carry on in his absence. But he missed the opportunity, and lost the support of his team in the process.

Good management is not a recent discovery

Of all the responsibilities central to the success of a manager, championing the cause of employees may be the greatest. Lao Tzu—the Chinese sage who proved that good management is not a recent invention—said as much in 600 BC. He said the key to success lies in creating an environment where others could be stars. "Fail to honor people," he wrote, "and they will fail to honor you." Although this advice has existed in one form or fashion for centuries, its application is still alien to many managers. A recent interview in a business magazine illustrates the point well.

The man interviewed in the article—a top executive for a Fortune 200 company—was asked about his philosophy on leadership and the "game" of business. "I know it isn't productive," he replied, "but when it comes time to cross the goal line, I want to be the person carrying the ball." One had to feel a little sorry for those employees who had to support this man's efforts. He reminded me of a quarterback we had in school—I'll call him Swag (short for "swagger")—who shared a similar point of view.

Like the Fortune 200 guy, Swag wanted to be the person carrying the ball when it came time to cross the goal line. His strategy was a simple one. He would give the ball to the halfback, a big bruising fellow with a talent for running over people, until the team got close to the goal line. At that point, he would call a "quarter-back sneak," a play that allows the quarterback to follow a blocker a short distance. By calling this play at the goal line, Swag scored all the points and received the resulting cheers. He was the star.

As Swag racked up touchdown after touchdown, his reputation grew. He was applauded and cheered at every turn. At first, the team was happy just to be winning. After a while, however, Swag's acclaim began to wear thin. Tired of doing the dirty work in the trenches so someone else could look good, Swag's teammates began letting things slip by...things like 250-pound tackles from the opposing team. Swag's once spotless jersey began needing a considerable amount of cleaning. Clueless as to the effect of his actions, Swag continued to call the quarterback sneak at the goal line. His season was ended prematurely by a vicious—unchecked—tackle.

Hogging the glory

In his interview, our Fortune 200 manager noted that his management philosophy was probably unproductive. He could have added selfish, arrogant, and grossly out of step with the needs and demands of today's work force. Failure to grasp the star-maker role of leadership in a hypercompetitive business environment may be the greatest mess-up a manager can make. Nevertheless, managers continue to call the quarterback sneak so they can hog the glory. Consider the following:

A talented young supervisor with an innovative concept for improving her department has her idea rejected by a critical manager. Later, the manager submits the idea to his superiors as his own and receives a citation and cash award for the savings generated.

A store manager of a retail chain arrives early and puts his initials on his employees' sales records. Although sales personnel receive no commission, when the records are reviewed at the home office, the manager gets the recognition for the work.

A manager in a brokerage firm replaces the cover of a report prepared by a subordinate and submits the contents to the board as his own. The report leads to a promotion.

These are not hypothetical examples. These are real-life occurrences shared by subordinates fed up with busting their tail ends for managers who hog the glory. Most are more than ready to let some bruiser take his best shot at their bosses.

Fumble!

A good example of failing to create stars was shared with me by the human resource director of a Midwest electronics firm. She told me of a young man in her company who had been selected to manage a troubled engineering department. The group he inherited, though capable of doing a good job, had never been very productive. Other managers had tried to get the department on the right track, but all had failed. Under the direction of the newest appointee, however, things changed. Whatever it was he had done, it had an immediate impact. Enthusiasm and activity increased sharply. Productivity jumped dramatically.

Several months after taking over the engineering group, the new manager met a fellow worker at the coffee pot. "Boy," she gushed, "your department really seems turned on. I can't believe how many projects you've already completed this quarter." Basking in this unexpected, heady praise from an attractive coworker, the manager succumbed to temptation. "Yeah," he replied, "this company never had a real engineering department until I came along."

News travels fast in a small company. It wasn't long before the engineering group heard about their manager's comment. Within a couple of days, they reverted to old, unproductive habits, and the "great turnaround" ran aground. Several months later, the manager responsible for "working miracles" in engineering was assigned to another division. Try as he would, he was no longer capable of motivating his group. The HR manager telling me the story concluded, "It was such a small mistake, but it had huge consequences."

There are clear parallels between this situation and the ones involving the Fortune 200 manager and my high school quarterback. All were involved in situations where the goal could not be accomplished without a capable team. All decided to hog the glory, and all suffered the consequences of that decision. Lester Thurow, Dean of the Sloan School of Business at MIT, said it best when he noted the importance of giving team members credit for the victory. "You have to give followers as well as leaders credit," he noted, "or everyone will refuse to be a team follower and will insist on being a team leader."

Turning failure into victory

1. Advise top management of your "star-maker" commitment. Let your boss know that your job, as you interpret it, is to develop, encourage, and champion the people working for you. If your department does well, your manager will be aware of your hand in it.

2. Remember that managing isn't about being the star. It's about facilitating—enabling others to do well. It means seeking opportunities to "hand the ball off" to other players. Achievement should have the fingerprints of the whole team on it, not just the manager's.

3. Look for opportunities to promote the efforts of your group. See yourself as a one-person public relations firm responsible for touting the efforts of your staff. Look for creative ways to honor those who make things happen. I like to give out Oscars (plastic ones!) for "best performances."

4. Remember that authentic managers never lose track of the need to serve. Make sure you're available to inform, train, counsel, guide, and support the efforts of your team. Don't let the pressures of the day's work keep you from investing in the future of your staff.

5. Take care to avoid a crisis of legitimacy with your staff by making sure your support and encouragement are free of any trace of manipulation. There's a fine line between championing the cause of people and using them selfishly.

Mess-Up No. 2

Failure to "keep the flame" by championing the company's beliefs and values.

"And if the bugler doesn't sound a clear call, how will the soldiers know they are being called to battle?"

—1 Corinthians, 14:8 (NLT)

One of my favorite Jack London works is a short story called "To Build a Fire." It tells about a man and his dog that starts off across Alaska on the Yukon Trail just as the hard winter sets in. Their journey is a difficult one, a frightful struggle against blinding snow and subfreezing temperatures. London writes that the dog followed "discouragingly," fully aware of the consequences of temperatures more than 70 degrees below zero. The dog follows not out of loyalty, but out of the belief that the man could provide warmth. The man not only had matches, but the ability to make a fire.

Keep the home fires burning

A number of years ago, I was involved in setting up a plant in Cumbernauld, Scotland. The company I represented was unusual in that it had an extraordinary commitment to its customers long before service became the latest corporate "discovery." One of the reasons that commitment was so high was the founder and president of the company, who made it a point to keep his passion for serving customers in front of our eyes. There was never a meeting convened that didn't begin with an exhortation from the president regarding service. Sometimes, at the beginning of the meeting, he would ask if the customer would benefit from our session. One time a manager answered, "No, not in any way that I can see." The owner gathered his papers, picked up his coffee and left, saying, "If it doesn't help the customer, we don't need it."

As we prepared to expand our business to another country, our greatest concern was whether this strategy could be translated to another culture. I remember being in Dublin one evening and sharing this concern with a manager from the Bank of Ireland. "I don't understand," he said, "how smiling at customers can make you guys so much more competitive." As we continued our conversation, I told the man that treating customers kindly was important, but that our customer service strategy went far beyond that. I then shared with him some stories of how our service had touched customers and shaped their view of our company. He replied, "I see, customer service is your ethos!"

An ethos (flame) of service

Ethos, a word that means distinguishing character or fundamental belief, was the perfect one to describe our company's commitment to customer service; it was our ethos. Finding a leader in the U.K. who shared our commitment to service, I realized, would be critical to our success. We needed someone who would feel that passion and embrace that belief as strongly as we did. As I interviewed candidate after candidate at the offices of the Scottish Development Agency in Glasgow, I began to feel our efforts would be in vain. I remember interviewing one manager and asking him to tell me what word his coworkers would use to describe his management style. "Exocet," he quickly replied. Puzzled, I asked why he would use the French guided missile as a symbol. He explained, "I fly to the target and blow it up." "Next!" I heard myself mutter under my breath.

With one candidate left, I was ready to concede defeat. The man, however, turned out to be exactly what we were looking for. Not only did he have a variety of skills ranging from sales to production, he spoke our language. When I asked him what he considered the essential ingredients for success in business, he quickly responded, "Quality products, quality people, and quality services." We hired the man immediately and made arrangements to bring him to our facility in the United States for training and further indoctrination in our philosophy and values. He spent two months absorbing our culture before leaving to open the U.K. plant.

On more than a few occasions he commented on the great symbolism we used to keep service in everyone's minds. His training completed, we held a reception to give him a big send-off. After opening several gifts from his new associates, the man offered some parting comments to our team. They were memorable. "I've lit a candle from the flame that burns so brightly here," he said. "I will care for it until I can safely place it in its new home, where others can benefit from its light and warmth."

The president of this company was a "keeper of the flame," but so were we. We found that each of us, as managers and leaders, could light our candles off his and take them back to our respective departments where our associates would repeat the process. If any of us failed to "keep the flame," the light would fail to reach the entire company. And when you are talking about service excellence, you must reach the entire company. The same is true for any value on which a company seeks to establish its distinction.

Protecting the flame

Every organization that achieves some degree of lasting success has well-defined values and beliefs—and managers who understand their critical purpose and champion their preservation. For some, those beliefs will center on service. For others, Six Sigma; still others, Lean Manufacturing; and so on. These beliefs and values will eventually coalesce into the critical success factors that define the direction the company will choose. But unless a flame is lit somewhere, that message may never reach the entire company.

At the end of London's story, the man crossing the Yukon Trail foolishly uses up his matches. Unable to provide warmth for his dog or himself, he perishes. At first, the dog sits patiently waiting for the man to build a fire. After a while, it decides the man can no longer give it what it wants, so it decides to leave. London writes, "A little longer it delayed, howling under the stars that leaped and danced and shown brightly in the cold sky. Then it turned and trotted up a trail in the direction of the camp it knew, where there were other fire-providers."

Unless managers become keepers of the flame, they run the risk of seeing employees wandering off in search of other sources of "warmth."

Turning failure into victory

1. Protect your flame from sudden drafts. There is much in the typical company experience that can snuff it out: cynicism, bias, envy, indifference—all can serve to extinguish the brightest of flames.

2. Identify your company's CSFs (Critical Success Factors), and keep them in front of the eyes of your staff. By presenting these factors on a regular, routine basis, managers fan them into vigorous flames.

3. Make sure that every employee has an opportunity to see the flame (hear the message) and light their candle. This means that new employees (or associates) must be exposed to the message early and often.

4. Understand that all candles must be lit to generate the brightest flame. Find out who's reluctant to "light up" and, if possible, why. If the reason is legitimate, deal with it. If not, invite the individual to look elsewhere for light. It's that important.

5. Model the behavior you expect. Keep your fire stoked! When the flame goes out at the top, it's not long before the whole organization "goes dark." Leadership is a top-down proposition.

Mess-Up No. 3

Failure to understand that the key ingredient in leadership is not power, but influence.

"The people are fashioned according to the example of their kings; and edicts are of less power than the life (example) of the ruler."

—Claudian, 365 B.C.

"Have you met our president?" the meeting planner asked. I indicated I had not, and she immediately took me by the arm and escorted me to where the president was talking with several others. "You're really going to be impressed," she whispered in my ear. "She's really special." The president, seeing us standing nearby, disengaged herself from the group and came over for introductions. "I loved your presentation," she said. "I can't remember ever taking so many notes." We chatted for a few minutes, with her asking for more detail on some of my points. After we left, my hostess asked if I had ever had a president take notes at one of my programs before. "Yes," I replied, "but only the good ones."

In that brief encounter, the president of this company had made a significant impact on me. I admit that I'm favorably impressed by people who speak kindly about my work, but this went beyond that. Even though I was there in my official capacity as a motivator and encourager, I found myself feeling pretty good about me! The first rule of salesmanship, I thought to myself, is that people buy not because they like you, but because they like themselves when they are around you. Although the woman had position power, what really moved mountains in her company was her ability to influence the people around her.

Are we finished?

A manager summons his employee into his office. As the employee enters, his boss rises to close the door behind him. Without waiting for the man to be seated, the manager asks why the employee had made some changes on a key account. "I felt that we had a better chance of getting the order with the changes," the employee replies. "Excuse me," the manager says, "but where does it say you can change my directions without my permission?" "I was just trying..." Before he could complete his sentence, the manager, his voice rising in anger, said, "Get this or get out. I run this department. It's my authority

that directs its efforts. Your job is to carry out my assignments, understand?" The worker rises to leave. "Just a
minute," the manager shouts, "I'm not through with you."
"No," the employee responds, "but I'm through with you."

This story, shared with me by the employee who experienced it, is an excellent illustration of management's
misunderstanding of where real power comes from. This
guy's manager assumed that because he had position (title)
power, he could use his authority to control his department. In reality, the man held considerably less power than
he thought. As Ken Blanchard, author of *Servant Leader*
notes, the real power in leadership today is influence, not
authority. The manager in the previous illustration discovered that control in today's workplace is largely an
illusion. In entirely different circumstances, another "manager" experienced a similar rejection of his authority.

The myth of position power

Just after the first Persian Gulf War, President George
H.W. Bush's approval rating reached an all-time high.
His reelection chances were so strong, many of the best
candidates in the opposition party decided not to run.
Within the space of a few months, however, the President's
approval rating began to fall. He appeared to be out of
touch with the needs of the common man. In November of
1992, his authority compromised by his inability to influence those he sought to lead, President Bush was asked
by the country to give up his responsibilities. In a position many call the most powerful in the world, the president was not able to exercise enough of it to keep his job.

The importance of influence as an ingredient of effective leadership is more important than ever. Today's worker,
having learned the concept of participative management,
is not inclined to return to autocratic methods. Managers
need to realize that power no longer comes with a title and
a corner office. Power, the ability to alter circumstances in
the lives of workers, is not so much something given as

granted. Unless workers choose to let power rest with you, you really do not have it, no matter what your title is. That's why influence is so critical.

The nature of influence

Through the years, influence has been described in ways that almost make it seem mystic. One definition describes it as a kind of spiritual or moral force. Others describe it as authority, prestige, or credibility. In a management sense, influence is the ability to secure a desired outcome without the apparent use of force or direct command. Influence arises from the confidence others have in the manager's ability to either take them where they want to go or demonstrate a better alternative.

People who are effective in influencing others seem to have a good understanding—consciously or otherwise—of the basic needs of people. Psychologists tell us that each of us has a deep-rooted need to be understood, to feel welcome, to feel comfortable, and to believe that our lives matter. People who are able to facilitate the acquisition of "satisfiers" will be able to exert the most influence.

As a seminar leader, my primary responsibility is to act as a facilitator. Although I have the authority of my client to conduct the programs, I'm aware that my ability to accomplish meaningful objectives is deeply rooted in my ability to influence my audience. Within a short period of time—experts say within two to three minutes—the majority of people in the room will make a decision as to whether or not to grant me the role of leader.

Leadership is granted

The beginning of my program is designed to connect with the needs of my audience as quickly as possible. I want them to feel welcome, comfortable, understood, and special. If successful, I will be able to exert some power to influence—if only for a few hours.

In the office environment, the ability to provide leadership is defined over a greater period of time. As a result, it's rooted in concepts and behaviors that take longer to cultivate. Some of those concepts and behaviors include:

- ❖ Personal prestige (generally associated with your success record).
- ❖ Personal credibility (how much trust you can generate).
- ❖ Technical credibility (your ability to comprehend and fix the problem).
- ❖ Personal vision (a clear idea of what "winning" looks like).
- ❖ Weight (the amount you have to "throw around" if necessary).
- ❖ Alliances (who you are able to influence that controls resources).
- ❖ Consultative capacity (the degree to which you seek the opinions of others).
- ❖ Communication skill (your talent for rational persuasion).
- ❖ Inspirational appeal (ability to "sell" your vision to others).

When most or all of the items on this list are in place, a manager can secure the power he or she needs to effect necessary changes. Without it, managers run the risk of losing the commitment and support of good employees who confer authority on those they perceive best qualified to use it.

Turning failure into victory

1. Understand that whereas management, the ability to get work done with and through other people, is more permanent, leadership has to be earned (granted) daily.
2. The ability to influence involves contact with other people. The personal touch makes the difference. Get

out of the office and circulate, using contacts with others as an opportunity to build personal credibility.

3. People are drawn to, and influenced by, the power of your beliefs. When you make contact with other people, use the art of conversation and storytelling to draw mental pictures of what you strongly believe in. Share your vision of the future often and with conviction.

4. Recognize and apply the key components of influence: listening to others, soliciting their opinions, making them feel wanted and needed. Look for opportunities daily to reinforce and supplement your "granted power."

5. People are most influenced by those who connect with their needs. Meet often with the people in your department to discover those needs individually, as well as collectively.

Mess-Up No. 4

Failure to occupy the land with character.

"People want to trust. They're hungry for it, but they're selective. They'll only give it to someone who, in good times or bad, always does the right thing."

—Jeffrey Immelt,
chairman of General Electric

In the annals of management history, no name rises higher or merits the title "guru" more than that of Peter Drucker. As a writer and management theorist, he is without peer. From his first book in 1939 to his latest work (he still averages a book a year), Drucker has penned over 10,000 pages on management and leadership. And that number doesn't include the thousands of articles he's written on the subject. As Jim Collins, author of *Good to Great*, notes, "Drucker occupies a rare quadrant of genius, being both highly prolific and remarkably insightful."

When Drucker was asked recently to put together a compendium of his work, he set out (with the assistance of Joseph Maciariello) to distill his books into 366 salient points. The result was *The Daily Drucker: 366 Days of Insight and Motivation for Getting the Right Things Done.* It offers a comprehensive survey of an important body of management theory. In writing my book, I gave considerable thought to which of my Mess-Ups merited "first spot." I felt the lead Mess-Up should be the one managers needed to consider most. I was sure Drucker had done the same, so I was anxious to get his book and see what met his criteria.

Drucker chose as his offering for January 1 (first spot), a clarion call for integrity in leadership. Because the whole message is conveyed in two short paragraphs, he gets straight to the point: The proof of a manager's sincerity and seriousness is revealed in his or her "uncompromising emphasis on integrity of character." It's only speculation, but I have little difficulty seeing Drucker telling Maciareillo, "Move this one to the top of the list."

Like Drucker, I believe the heart and soul of management and leadership is the strength and depth of one's character. In the pages that follow, I've offered nearly 300 pieces of advice for "turning failure into victory." Each, in some form or fashion, requires an act of character to carry it out. Character is what powers a manager's "people" decisions.

Above all else

Norman Schwarzkopf, the charismatic general who led coalition forces in Desert Storm, once defined leadership as a potent combination of strategy and character. "If you have to be without one," he said, "be without the strategy." Schwartzkopf understood the importance of Robert Frost's admonition to "occupy the land with character." While it's important to have a viable plan (strategy), it's vital to remember that belief in the plan is often dependent on belief in the planner. That belief is shaped, more than anything else, by how that person comports herself day-by-day.

Generally speaking, the first thing people think about when they think of character is what I like to call the HIT list: honesty, integrity, and truth-telling. When it comes to the character of managers and leaders, those things are "table stakes," the minimum needed to get in the game. If anyone seeks to lead others, to attempt to influence attitudes, opinions, and behavior, more will be required of their character then simply telling the truth (although that's not a bad place to start). Occupying the land with character paints a larger picture of service, courage, compassion, wisdom, fortitude, and more.

As noted, each piece of advice offered in this book is powered by an act of character. Even the motives behind them are shaped by the leader's character. Consider these points covered in the Mess-Ups that follow:

❖ Listening, the willingness to give another person your full and undivided attention, is an act of character. Many believe it to be the primary transmitter of integrity.

❖ Accountability, the courage to set meaningful and challenging goals, then holding every member equally responsible for doing their part, is an act of character.

❖ Honoring the mini-contracts ("my door is always open") executed daily with employees is an act of character.

❖ Offering positive reinforcement to an employee with no other motive than to acknowledge and honor their contribution is an act of character.

❖ Communicating in an open and timely fashion with employees during times of change and uncertainty is an act of character.

❖ Providing employees with the resources (time, money, and training) needed to succeed in their assignments is an act of character.

Making decisions with the best interests of your customers in mind is an act of character.

Occupying the land with character as a manager and leader means carrying out your responsibilities day by day and hour by hour in such a way as to insure they are in the best interests of followers. It means developing a servant (others-directed) mentality in leadership. Here are a few short examples of how a leader's character was revealed in day-by-day affairs.

Character in adversity

Although character deals with issues of integrity and proper behavior, it also deals with a person's capacity to respond to adversity. When my father was a boy, he accompanied his mother on an ocean voyage from New York to Bremen, Germany. On the return trip, their vessel encountered one of the worst storms of that era. As the ship tossed back and forth between crashing waves, frightened passengers grabbed railings along the hallways and clutched them for dear life. I asked my dad if he was scared too. "I was at first," he said, "then I saw the captain." In the midst of all the turmoil, the ship's captain was seen leisurely walking about the deck with hands clasped behind his back. "I was comforted by his presence and confidence," my father told me.

Selfless acts

When my wife's mother died of cancer after a lengthy illness, we were surprised to see the CEO of her company come to the visitation. It was a Sunday afternoon, time most of us guard jealousy, and he had just completed a lengthy drive to get there. He was there less than an hour because of pressing deadlines to meet in the morning. Nevertheless, he considered it important enough to invest seven hours of his valuable time to demonstrate his regard and concern for an employee. As Rudy Giuliani says, "Weddings are optional. Funerals are mandatory." Especially for leaders of character.

Selfless choices

According to the Old Testament, when Solomon ascended to the throne at the death of King David, God appeared to him in a dream and offered to grant him anything he asked for. Imagine the possibilities that lay before this young leader! He could have asked for a long life, riches beyond imagination, power to control others, or the endless praise and admiration of followers. His response, recorded in II Chronicles, was a selfless one: "Give me wisdom and knowledge," he said, "to rule them (followers) properly." Solomon's first decision as a leader was an others-directed act of character.

Compassion and humility

On the wall in my office is a copy of a letter written by Abraham Lincoln to Lydia Bixby on November 21, 1864 to acknowledge the death of her sons in the war. Lincoln wrote, "I feel how weak and fruitless must be any word of mine which would attempt to beguile you from the grief of a loss so overwhelming." Part of Lincoln's character was this marvelous blend of compassion and humility revealed in his handwritten letter. Even though he was president and commander in chief of the military, Lincoln felt his words would be "weak and fruitless." Taking time to connect with this woman's grief was an act of compassion and humility...and character.

As Drucker notes, employees will forgive a great deal: Incompetence, ignorance, insensitivity, or even bad manners. "They will not forgive a lack of integrity," Drucker writes, "nor will they forgive higher management for choosing him." Who you are impacts how you lead, and that's something employees can figure out pretty quickly.

Turning failure into victory

Here are five acts of character drawn from our illustrations that will strengthen relationships with workers and followers:

1. When storms hit, stroll the deck. In the midst of strife and difficulty, leaders and managers of character need to be both visible and accessible (think Rudy Giuliani). When managers "get scarce" in times of trouble (change, crisis, downsizing, and so on), followers lose confidence in their ability to lead.

2. Strengthen character daily. Read about men and women of great resolve and courage who were able to achieve extraordinary things. Immerse yourself daily in quotes and stories that inspire and provide a template for leadership. I recommend the works of O.S. Marden.

3. Remember that leadership is first and foremost an act of service. Look for opportunities to become more "others directed" in your work. Look for opportunities to extend yourself personally to your team, to connect with the human element of management. History will not acknowledge your success unless it contains contribution as well.

4. Never underestimate the power of a handwritten note of concern or appreciation. Through the years, I've received thousands of e-mails, many offering positive feedback on my work. Although appreciated, most were deleted. Handwritten notes, however, were retained and placed in a file I review often.

5. Begin where you are. Many managers and leaders have taken a tumble off the "character path" during their careers, most minor missteps. But honor is recoverable, and it's never too late to become the person you might have been.

Part 2:
Communication

Mess-Up No. 5

Failure to understand that the most powerful and persuasive thing a manager can do is listen.

"Speech is a joint game between the talker and the listener against the forces of confusion. Unless both make the effort, interpersonal communication is quite hopeless."

—Norman Weiner, Ph.D.,
business consultant

"Will you listen to me?!" I turned to see who was doing the shouting and saw a mother sternly reprimanding her preschooler. Exasperated at trying to get her daughter's attention, her frustration gushed out. I wondered how many employees have wanted to do the same thing with their managers. I mean, just grab them by the shoulders, give them a big shake and shout in their face, "Will you listen to me?!" It reminded me of an encounter not too long ago I had with a subordinate.

Worth the effort

I was busily working at my desk, trying to complete an important report, when Jane walked in and asked if she could talk to me. "Sure," I replied, continuing to work on my project. I continued for a minute before I realized Jane was not speaking. When I looked up, I saw that she had taken a seat and was waiting patiently for me to finish. "Go ahead," I urged, still focusing my attention else-where. "I'll wait," she answered. "It's okay," I said, "I'm listening." "No, you're not," she replied. Her comment caught me by surprise. I put down my pen and said, "You have my full attention." "Good," she said, "I'm worth it."

Listening is one of the most powerful things we do as human beings—when we do it, that is. Unfortunately, most of us aren't very good at it. When you consider the range of emotions that are affected by listening, you won-der why it wasn't covered in school with the same em-phasis as science and math. No one should graduate without taking Listening Skills 101. It's basic, it's crucial, and it's ignored. Listening, one of the most persuasive (yes, persuasive) things a person can do, is a skill few managers have mastered. Studies indicate most manag-ers listen at an extraordinary low rate of effectiveness.

The art of persuasion

Few will disagree that the ability to persuade others is a key element of successful management. Many, how-ever, will not be as easily convinced that listening is one of the most effective tools in the process. "How can I per-suade without talking?" they want to know. I'm not sug-gesting that persuasion can be accomplished without conveying your ideas. I am saying that speaking alone will not change many minds. People have to be listened to in order to believe they have worth and value, and that they're not just a tool for accomplishing corporate goals.

When we choose to listen to others, we give them one of our most cherished resources—our time. This alone is a powerful symbol of our intentions toward them. By lis-tening, we affirm their worth and state in obvious terms that they matter. In the process, we fulfill a couple of their basic human needs—the need to be understood and the need to feel important. When people have their needs met by someone, they are much more likely to listen to the plans of that person. As a result, good listening skills can be persuasive.

Some management listening sins

Communication (especially the listening part) is filled with opportunities for misunderstanding and confusion for today's manager. During my management development seminars, I always ask participants to generate a list of their favorite management "listening sins." Surprisingly, the list varies little from group to group. The 10 most frequently mentioned examples given include:

❖ Multitasking (number-one answer).

❖ Doesn't smile when we talk.

❖ Never really looks at me.

❖ Always changes the subject.

❖ Allows interruptions.

❖ Never lets me complete a thought.

❖ Fidgets, seems irritated.

❖ Takes an awful lot of notes.

❖ Tries to turn around what I say.

❖ Makes me feel insignificant.

As you can see, there are a lot of emotions tied up in the act of listening. Do it well, and the other person feels good about themselves and their ideas. Do it poorly, and the emotions range from resentment to outright anger.

Can you hear me now?

A group of weary people filed into the conference room on Friday morning for their company's weekly team meeting designed to improve communication between management and staff. The communication, such as it was, consisted of the president telling them they needed to work harder and bill more hours. The session concluded each week with the presentation of the president's Q-Tip Award to acknowledge an individual act of quality.

Although the meeting had originated as a result of an employee survey giving poor marks to leadership on communication, the session had devolved into an opportunity for the president and other managers to lecture the staff for an hour each week. The Q-Tip Award was added so they could "end on a positive note." After a particularly one-sided session had ended with the presentation of the giant swab, the winner was heard to quip, "If they had ears to match this Q-Tip, maybe they could hear our cries for help."

Return on investment

The management and leadership benefits of effective listening are huge. It helps raise the self-esteem of the speaker. It helps to prime the pump, assuring the manager of the continued flow of much-needed information and ideas. It helps cement the relationship between the speaker and listener. It helps to prevent mistakes that often occur when communication breaks down.

Becoming an effective listener requires skill and knowledge. The primary factor determining your level of success as a listener is your desire—your attitude toward the people and the process. An effective leader in today's business environment should be spending as much as 80 percent of his or her time actively listening to people—employees, customers, suppliers, and peers. And that's just the people at work!

Turning failure into victory

Although communication is a complex process, here's a simple formula that might help you focus on the key ingredients of effective listening. I call it the P.O.W.E.R. listening model.

Step 1: Listen Perceptively. Listening perceptively involves listening with senses other than vision. Webster defines perception as characterized by understanding and insight. What I'm suggesting is the need to listen between the words for feeling and emotion. A well-known study on the communication of attitude by Dr. Albert Mahrabian at UCLA says that 38 percent of what we interpret is based on the *tone* in which something is said. Listening perceptively requires that special attention be given to the tone of voice used, what is left unspoken, and what is implied.

Step 2: Be *O*bservant. Returning again to Mahrabian's study, 55 percent of communication is based on what people see. The P.O.W.E.R. listener watches the speaker for additional information. I remember watching the CEO of a major healthcare organization during an interview on television. He was being questioned about some alleged improprieties. Although his words stated otherwise, his mannerisms and movement seemed to be saying, "I'm not coming clean on this issue!"

Step 3: Be *W*illing. This step actually belongs at the beginning because all effective listening begins with our commitment to take part in the conversation. The act of listening may well be one of the most unnatural acts we perform. Setting aside our own needs and agenda in favor of someone else's runs contrary to basic human nature. That's why good listening requires a deliberate effort to make it work.

Step 4: Be *E*ngaged. Engaged in my model implies a level of connectedness with the speaker through the use of active feedback. Let me illustrate.

I was recently speaking on the phone with a colleague who never made a sound while I was speaking. Even when I paused, the silence continued! After an awkward pause I asked, "Are you there?" "Yes," he replied, "Something you said caught my attention and I was thinking about it." Without being aware, my friend had disconnected me. Being engaged as a listener means giving the speaker feedback to let him or her know you're involved.

Step 5: Be *R*espectful. By giving respect, a listener dignifies the speaker. When I failed to give the lady in my opening illustration my full attention, I had inadvertently treated her with a lack of respect. Listening respectfully means providing the speaker with focused attention, time to speak without interruptions, and not letting your mind race ahead to form a reply.

Becoming a P.O.W.E.R. listener requires a real commitment. But if you wish to become a more effective manager and leader, you're wasting your time if you fail to master this skill. It's the primary way a manager conveys integrity.

■

Mess-Up No. 6

Failure to recognize the silent communication of management.

"A man without a smiling face ought not to open a shop."

—Chinese proverb

Michelle was at the copier when I approached, mindlessly whistling a tune I'd heard on the radio. "I'm glad to see you're in a good mood today," she said. "Why's that?" I asked. "When you're in a good mood," she replied, "the whole department is in a good mood." "Does the opposite apply?" I asked jokingly. As she started to leave she replied, "Well, when you're not smiling everybody wonders what they've done wrong." As she left, I remembered a comment my pastor recently had made in a sermon. "When mama ain't happy," he said, "ain't nobody happy!" I wondered if that applied to managers as well.

That evening, I shared my associate's comments with my wife. To my surprise, she agreed with Michelle. Even my teenage daughter, listening in on the conversation, agreed with the opposition. "And," she added, "when you don't smile, you look kind of mad." That night I stood in front of the mirror making an assortment of faces to see what they meant. I finally chose a look I thought to be neutral. It took me by surprise. "Gee," I thought, "I do look mad."

Everything sends a message

Few managers are aware of the nonverbal impact they have on the thoughts and opinions of their employees. Like it or not, there can be no contact between worker and manager that does not result in the communication of a feeling or attitude. Your facial expression, how you walk, how and where you sit in a meeting, what you wear—all serve to define your attitude, especially if it's a bad one.

A bad attitude is the worst thing that can happen to a group of people, especially if that attitude belongs to a manager. I ran into a friend recently who works for a manager whose demeanor permeates every aspect of his department, and not in a positive way. She called him "the monster" and said he made life miserable for everyone. She recalled being summoned into his office once and having to wait 10 minutes—in silence—while he finished writing a memo. I asked her what the purpose of the meeting was. "He gave me a raise," she said.

When you talk about managers with a negative attitude, the illustration in the preceding paragraph is probably close to most people's perceptions. In reality, most managers convey negative signals in more subtle ways. After listening to my friend complain at length about her boss, it dawned on me that she had said little about the man's actual words. Most of her comments had been directed at a range of behaviors most easily classified as nonverbal. It occurred to me that this "monster" may have been a competent manager, but one who understood little about silent communication.

Putting on a game face

The president of a bank once asked me to sit in on a department meeting led by one of his top managers. There had been a number of complaints from the man's staff about his attitude. "He's a very competent person," the president noted, "but his people come out of his meetings totally frustrated." He went on to say that the most common complaint against the manager was his apparent indifference. His staff was reacting with resentment and frustration. With that kind of an introduction, I couldn't wait to see the guy in action.

The meeting began as scheduled, and it wasn't long before I saw what this manager's employees were talking about. The man was sending a variety of nonverbal signals, beginning with his posture. He sat semi-slumped in his chair at the head of the table, obscuring a portion of his face with his hand. During the meeting, he made little eye contact with other participants, preferring to keep his gaze fixed on the table in front of him. He took no notes and offered no comments. He didn't even bother to pick up the handouts placed in front of him. Regardless of the topic, his reaction—controlled indifference—remained the same.

I later learned this man was an avid poker player. He not only played regularly, he was a student of the game. Without being aware of it, this manager was taking his game face into every meeting he attended. His lack of expression, which served him well in poker, was dealing him a "bad hand" in relationships with employees.

As managers, we are charged with the responsibility of increasing productivity, raising morale and insuring job satisfaction to some degree every day. To do that successfully requires a keen awareness of all our communications—silent as well as spoken.

Turning failure into victory

1. Recognize that everything you do, as a manager, sends a message. Where you sit, whom you talk to, what you wear all speak volumes. Take these things into consideration and make them work for, not against, you.

2. Identify your silent signals. Tactfully ask some employees you trust what nonverbal messages you send that they may regard as confusing or negative. The only problems you can solve are the ones you know about, so go ahead and ask!

3. Remember that a smile can empower others and raise productivity. This is not an invitation to practice phoniness, but to do a better job of "facial management." Most managers fail to smile simply because they forget to!

4. Take a moment at the beginning of each day to strategically plan the nonverbal impact you want to have on your organization—in meetings, in your office, or at the coffee pot. Remember, the attitude of your group is in your hands.

5. Model the behavior you expect. If you want an organization that operates without negativity, indifference, and fear, then communicate that message verbally and nonverbally. Shaping the attitudes of others is part of your job as a manager.

Mess-Up No. 7

Failure to bridge the "great divide."

"Men are never so likely to settle a question rightly as when they discuss it freely."

—Thomas B. Macaulay, 19th-century
English statesman and historian

Of all the management Mess-Ups shared in this book, this one is uniquely my own. In a way, I'm glad it occurred. It served as a timely reminder that these mistakes are easy to commit, even if you're working hard at trying to avoid them. This illustration shows just how easy it is to get caught up in your own agenda and your own view of a problem, forgetting how that same problem looks from another perspective (or department).

The company for which I was working—a small manufacturer of electronic components—was experiencing many of the problems associated with rapid growth. Rush shipments, sudden schedule changes and increased workloads had served to put everyone on edge. While this was going on, I had succeeded in selling the company on the idea of investing $250,000 on a new advertising campaign based on the company's ability to perform. "When others can't or won't," the ad proclaimed, "we CAN and WILL!" In a market where precious little is predictable, our theme of flexibility and responsiveness succeeded in drawing attention.

Unfortunately, the attention it drew was not always productive. It seemed that every buyer who had failed to order parts on time expected our company to bail them out. Every materials manager, whose dock-to-stock initiative came up short, looked to us to rectify it. On more than a few occasions, our customer service reps had to go back to production to negotiate expedited delivery dates. These meetings grew more intense, and often erupted into shouting matches. Workers, already burdened with a heavy load, were being asked to work more and more overtime. We began to hear comments up front that the "guys in the back" were not team players. "We're telling the customer we can," one rep noted, "and they're telling us we can't."

Our top management group met to discuss the problem, and decided that the guys in the back needed to know what was on the line. We decided to hold a company-wide meeting to let everyone know about our new $250,000 advertising commitment, and to tell them how important it was for us to "pull together as a team." As the vice president of marketing and author of the ad campaign, I was elected to present the program to the staff. I decided to be creative and used this dramatic story to illustrate my point.

A little teamwork

During the Vietnam War, four men were sent out in a jeep on patrol. As they were driving along, they suddenly came under enemy fire. All four men jumped from the vehicle and found cover in nearby fields. As they lay there, the master sergeant began to consider the alternatives. *If we just stay here*, he thought, *we'll be captured. If we jump in the jeep and drive on, we'll just be going deeper into enemy territory.* He finally decided that the best idea was to turn the jeep around and head back to camp. The problem was, there was no room to turn around.

After giving it further thought, the sergeant came upon the idea of picking the jeep up and turning it around. *If everybody believes we can do it*, he thought, *then we can.* He then polled his troops to see if they believed it could be done. They did. He assigned each a corner of the jeep (good management!), then gave a command. On his shout, the four men rushed to the jeep, picked it up and turned it around, then jumped in, and drove safely back to camp.

Meanwhile, back at the ranch

The message of the story was teamwork, and it went well, from my perspective. I told it with enthusiasm, passion, and high drama. When I finished, even the CEO of the company was impressed. After telling the story, I launched into an enthusiastic presentation of our new advertising campaign. "Over the next 12 months," I gushed, "we'll be spending nearly $250,000 to promote our company." I told them how important it was, in order to prevent a crisis of legitimacy, to make sure we met our promises. "It will take," I concluded, "the same commitment and effort it took those four soldiers on the battlefield in Vietnam." I sat down with one thought in my mind: *Darn, I'm good!*

The results of my brilliant presentation were quick in coming. Things went from bad to awful. They were nearly at the point of exploding, when I met one of our production people at the coffee pot. Known for her outspoken candor, she told me in no uncertain terms what she thought of my presentation. "I wish you had never told us about that advertising thing," she said. "Why?" I asked. "What we really need," she said, "are more people to put the parts together." As she walked out of the room she added, "We've kissed off any hope of getting a raise this year. We figure it will go to pay for advertising."

The feedback I received, as painful as it was, was welcome. By being honest with me, the production worker reminded me that there can be more than one interpretation to a message. I thought I was giving them a vision of our future, assuring them that the company was doing what was necessary to make it grow and secure our jobs. Unfortunately, they were in another place. The feelings they brought to the meeting included resentment (too much work, not enough money) and a lack of appreciation. My presentation was seen as manipulation, a way to get them to do more while the people up front were "cashing in."

A meeting of the minds

Once the problem surfaced, we launched a program to establish regular, ongoing communication between the various departments. Monthly manager's meetings were implemented to ensure better communication and coordination of the various department heads. We began to encourage more communication between staff members as well, asking for feedback *before* decisions were being made. One change that yielded unexpected results wasn't directed at the problem at all. In an effort to gain extra production space, a rearrangement of the office brought production into closer proximity with administration. By removing walls—figurative as well as real—we were able to establish cross-functional interaction that improved both morale and productivity.

Turning failure into victory

1. Before beginning any new program to deal with friction or other problems, bring all parties together to discuss the ground rules. Let everyone know that the objective is not to find fault, but to surface solutions.

2. Avoid emotionally charged issues until you've established a working relationship with each other. Deal first with those problems you have a good chance of solving together.

3. Establish regular (but informal) meeting opportunities between the various departments. One company I work with has a "Morning Huddle," a brief 10 minute session to target the most important objectives of the day.

4. Advise managers of other departments of any decisions under consideration that might affect their areas. Remember, people don't like surprises when it comes to doing their jobs!

5. Encourage exchange sessions where members from other departments tell about their responsibilities. Be sure to include strategy and objectives as well as job descriptions.

Mess-Up No. 8

Failure to understand that the "GrapeNet" is still the most powerful means of communication in business.

"E-mail is quick, but not as quick as the boss's secretary."

—Anonymous

"Have you heard the latest?" a young sales clerk asked during her lunch break. "I hate to ask," another replied. "I just heard they're going to pay the holiday help $7 an hour," the first continued. Several other employees, also sales clerks, joined the group. Because most of these workers, known as permanent part-timers, were making less than $7 an hour, the salary of the new hires became a hot topic. Before long, everyone agreed they were getting stepped on and that each would be looking for someplace else to work. "There are 125 stores in this mall," one lady said, "and they're all hiring." Before long the word reached personnel. "Have you heard the latest?" one manager asked another. "I hate to ask," the other responded.

Winner and still champion...

BlackBerries and Bluetooth technology are making information available worldwide with extraordinary speed to anyone with access to a PDA, cell phone, or laptop computer. Although awesome in its capabilities, technology comes in a distant second to the fastest form of communication in any organization—the "GrapeNet" (the office grapevine). Unlike the Internet, which is dependent on the use of a modem, the GrapeNet can be accessed anywhere, anytime. GrapeNet terminals include coffee pots, lunchrooms, break areas—anywhere people congregate, socialize, and exchange information.

With the GrapeNet, people can be online and surfing before the average computer has had the time to boot up. Some of the more commonly visited Websites include:

- ❖ Haveyouheard.com.
- ❖ Frustration.com.
- ❖ Uncertainty.com.
- ❖ Salarygripe.com.
- ❖ Unconfirmedrumor.com.
- ❖ Gotfired.com.
- ❖ Downsizeworry.com.
- ❖ Misinformed.com.
- ❖ Inthedark.com.
- ❖ Resentment.com.
- ❖ Nobonusthisyear.com.

The average surfer on the GrapeNet can hyperlink from site to site with mind-numbing speed. In a world looking to technology to facilitate its complex communication needs, the office grapevine has yet to be matched. How many systems do you know of that exist today in the same basic form they did in biblical times?

Information via the grapevine—an informal communication system existing in every organization—dates back to Roman times when messages (we call it graffiti) were written on ancient walls. Stories are told about elaborate grapevines formed in concentration camps in World War II that enabled families to stay in touch.

During the Vietnam War, where prisoners were often denied face-to-face contact with each other, tapping replaced words as soldiers found ways to exchange information. It's not surprising then, that most companies have a robust, fully functional grapevine system in place. In larger organizations, there are multiple grapevines crisscrossing each other like complex fiber optic networks. Studies indicate that, due to the vast amount of change confronting business today, grapevines are functioning at the highest level ever.

The case for the grapevine

Although a friend of mine calls it the "GRIPEvine," the office grapevine is an important and useful tool for managers who understand how and why it works. Managers who use it most effectively are those who accept it not as a necessary evil, but as a normal and natural channel for sharing information on an informal basis. When a company is facing a period of uncertainty, or is considering major changes in its operations, the grapevine can be used effectively by management to get information to the troops. Granted, that information sometimes gets distorted, but studies indicate the grapevine is accurate more often than not.

Managers who make the grapevine work for them understand its purpose. They know that grapevines exist because people have a need for information. Smart managers are skilled at preserving the medium while cleaning up the accuracy of the message, and they know when and how to use it to keep people informed. "Gossip is the only thing that travels faster than the speed of light," says Joel Deluca, author of *Political Savvy*. "To help your career, you need to make sure you're part of the lightning rod that catches that information."

Turning failure into victory

1. Anticipate the need for information. Grapevines are most active in companies that do not communicate regularly with their employees. In the absence of information, employees will create their own. Learn to anticipate the times when more—not less—information is needed, and be prepared to provide it.

2. Make sure everyone understands that they are ultimately responsible for the information they load onto the system. Find out who the "frequent fliers" are and let them know they will be held responsible for the validity of the data "loaded."

3. Understand that information "uploaded" to the grapevine is often distorted by the emotions of unhappy employees. When you detect false information, immediately set the record straight.

4. Anticipate the periods of high activity generally associated with planned changes. Make an effort during these periods to increase more traditional forms of communication. The grapevine should supplement more reliable forms of communication, not replace them.

5. Tune in, listen up. Effective managers never underestimate the power of the grapevine. Find reliable sources to keep you informed. Make it a point to take breaks or join coworkers for lunch. As previously noted, the only problems you can solve are the ones you know about.

Part 3:
Motivation

Mess-Up No. 9

Failure to understand that employment is a marketing transaction monitored daily.

"You have been weighed on the balances and have failed the test."

—Daniel 5:27 (NLT)

If you believe in getting your money's worth, you would appreciate my daughter. She's a shopping whiz. If there is a bargain anywhere within a 50-mile radius of her home, she'll find it. Each Sunday she carefully studies the ads and lays out her shopping strategy. She and her friends compare notes and keep each other informed on the best bargains. Suitably prepared, she sets out to "browse the stores." She will only make a purchase when she believes the value she must give up (her hard earned money) is exceeded by the value she expects to receive. Unless it's a good deal, she just won't buy. Not surprisingly, she's made some pretty smart purchases.

By definition, a marketing transaction is one value exchanged for another. Smart buyers refuse to part with their value (usually money) unless they believe they will receive equal or greater value in return. The key word here is "believe." It's a rather mystical judgment we some-how make regarding a product's usefulness. It's hard to describe, but it's very real. It's a perception based many times on personal judgment, feeling, and good old intuition.

Employees shop for good deals, too

A strong case can be made that employment is noth-ing more than a marketing transaction. For example, when does an employer choose to extend an offer to a job can-didate? When that employer perceives that the value—contribution—they will receive will offset the cost of employment (more on this later). When does the em-ployee choose to accept the company's offer? When he feels the value he expects to receive will meet or ex-ceed what he gives in return. Here's an example of how this scenario might play out.

Suppose you were interviewing for a position. The whole purpose of a job interview is to uncover each other's values. I'm not talking about beliefs or morals here. I'm talking about what you have to offer a pro-spective employer in terms of marketable skills and talents, as well as what the employer has to offer you. Before your meeting with your prospective employer, you did a personal audit to see what you had to offer. You even put some of it down in chronological order on fancy paper (a little marketing never hurt). You were more persuasive in presenting your values than this, but here's what you basically believe you have to offer:

- Knowledge.
- Education.
- Training.
- Experience.
- Loyalty.
- Attitude.
- Commitment.
- Time.
- Integrity.
- Enthusiasm.

After an hour or so of examining your "product," your potential boss feels she has a pretty good handle on your overall worth. As a matter of fact, she's pretty excited about the possibility of adding you to the team! She's now looking over her list to see how her company's values stack up. Here's what her company will offer:

- Salary.
- Benefits.
- Loyalty.
- Commitment.
- Education program.
- Advancement.
- Stable employment.
- Praise/recognition.
- Meaningful work.
- Good reputation.
- Flextime.
- Childcare.

If the benefits of the company are weighed against those of the applicant, you would discover the scales pretty much balanced. Because the value each party feels it must give up is met or exceeded by what each expects to receive, an employment agreement is possible. Here's how the company might express its offer.

"Bill, we're impressed with what you have to offer Mega Computer. We'd like you to accept our offer to become the logistics manager for our new distribution center. If you accept, we'll give you an excellent starting salary with a review in 90 days. In addition, we want to invest in your future. After you've had an opportunity to get familiar with our operation, we're going to send you to the Swiss School of Management Development in Zurich. What do you say?"

What do you say? You jump on the offer! It's everything you hoped to get and then some.

For the first few months, you go all out for Mega Computer. You want your new employer to feel it got a great deal when it hired you. Ninety days later, you are pleased with your contribution and expect to be called into your boss's office for some praise and raise action. You've learned the operation quickly and fully expect an increase in salary and a plane ticket to Zurich. But nothing happens. At first you assume everyone is too busy to take time for your review. After six months, however, you feel you're being ignored. You make an appointment to meet with your boss to see where things stand.

"I'm glad you stopped by, Bill," your boss says, "I've been meaning to talk to you." "I know you're busy," you start awkwardly, "but some of the things I was promised when I was hired haven't been done." "Like what?" your boss asks defensively. "Well," you reply, "I was supposed to get a salary review after three months. And I was supposed to go to Switzerland for some management training. As far as I can see, I've done all that was asked of me and then some." "My goodness," your boss gushes, "you've done a terrific job! You're one of my best people." "Well," you ask, not sure where this is headed, "what about my raise?"

The bottom line

What you then learn from your boss is that things have not been going well for Mega Computers. You're told that an informal salary freeze is in effect and that you will not be getting the raise as promised. When you ask about Zurich, you learn that corporate education programs have been suspended until further notice. You are assured, however, that you are a real asset to the company and told you should hang in there for a few more months.

Remember, this started out as a marketing transaction with scales in balance. But the scales are no longer in balance; the employer has removed significant values from its side of the trays. What do you do? If you let things progress as they are, you'll feel like a fool for giving more than you believe you will receive in return. A bad bargain is emerging, and your choices are simple. You can either quit or do what the vast majority of workers do—bring the scales *back in balance* by reducing your value until it lines up with your perception of equity. Here's how it works. You used to come in early and work late. Your car was frequently in the parking lot on Saturdays and Sundays. Now you work the minimum needed to hang onto your job. Your enthusiasm, once high and contagious, is no longer high. But it's still contagious. You complain to everyone. You contribute less and less until you feel you have finally brought your values in line with those of the company. In your mind you are not under-performing. You are just making sure your company gets what it's paying for. It's your perception, but it's the one that counts.

Balancing the scales

A number of points can be drawn from this illustration, but the main one is this: Employment is a marketing transaction between two parties who exchange values in an attempt to get a good bargain. From the time of hire on, the employee will check the balance daily to see if it's still a good deal. Good management means making sure employees feel good about their investment—not every six months, but *every day*.

After a seminar recently, a man came up and shared a conversation he had with an employee. He had just given her a raise and told her what an asset she was to the company. "You know," the employee told him, "my work ethic has remained unchanged over the last 10 years. I worked very hard for each of my previous employers. But you're the first to really reward my effort." I asked the man what he thought the key point of the story was. He replied, "That it was her first raise?" I told him he was partially correct. The real key was that she had found her deals with her previous employers to be wanting. She had resigned previous jobs simply because, in her evaluation, they had turned into bad bargains.

Turning failure into victory

1. Accept the fact that employment is a marketing transaction and that you, as a manager, are responsible for keeping the scales balanced. Periodically review the deal to make sure it is still good for both parties.

2. Schedule regular opportunities to meet with employees to see if they are satisfied with the deal they are getting. Employee satisfaction surveys are good tools for checking corporate "balances," but not as good as "one-on-ones."

3. Avoid a crisis of legitimacy with your employees. Make sure you do not raise expectations beyond what you and your company are able to deliver. If anything put on the table is less than a certainty, make sure that is understood.

4. Look for ways to add value. Remember the "baker's dozen"? Everybody wants the thrill of getting a little more than they bargained for. The best employee will be the one pleasantly surprised on occasion by his or her employer.

5. Accept the fact that employees will occasionally shop around for better offers. If you lose an employee, make sure it's because they found a great deal somewhere else. You should never lose a valued employee to an average offer.

Mess-Up No. 10

Failure to make the people we deal with— customers and employees—feel important.

"Every customer is a special individual who wants to be treated as such. He has his own unique personality, wants, and reasons for buying. And to the extent that you treat him as someone special...he will continue to be your customer."

—Michael LeBoeuf,
How to Win Customers and Keep Them for Life

When Dana opened her pay envelope and examined her check, she thought it didn't look right. During lunch, she got out her calculator and figured she had been paid only $14.50 an hour, instead of the $14.75 she should have received. She went to the company's personnel department to get the problem corrected. Instead of addressing the problem, the assistant in the personnel department said she'd look into it when she had the time. When Dana asked to speak to the personnel manager she was told that the manager doesn't deal with "little stuff" like this.

This company has a real problem. In a business that relies heavily on part-time help from college students to staff its departments, they've developed a reputation for treating these people with indifference and disrespect. For a long time the prevailing wisdom seemed to be that if a part-timer got mad and left, they would just hire another. With a turnover rate running well ahead of applicants, however, the pool of available workers had suddenly dried up. Regular meetings are now being held with managers to teach them how to make employees feel valued.

A stark contrast

When it comes to making people feel special, few people do a better job of it than country music superstar Garth Brooks. Brooks, who holds a marketing degree from Oklahoma State University, is a manager who believes in making both employees and customers feel special. Before his surprising retirement, I took my family to see him in concert in Cincinnati and was impressed that he not only introduced his band, but his lighting and stage crew as well. His truck driver even got a standing ovation when Brooks brought him on stage to be introduced to the audience. Do you think that was a motivating moment for that employee?

Brooks's reputation for connecting with his customers is even greater. During his concert, fans were constantly offering flowers. Each time Brooks accepted their offerings (usually during a song), he took the flowers to an area in the center of his stage and carefully placed them in a row. In concluding his concert, he gathered the flowers and held them during his final number, then carried them offstage with him. By treating the flowers with care, Brooks sent a clear message of appreciation to the adoring "customers" (Brooks's term for his fans) who brought them. By honoring their actions, he made them, and all his other fans, feel special.

A basic need

Psychologists tell us that all humans have four basic needs: the need to feel comfortable, the need to be understood, the need to feel welcome, and the need to feel important. Marketing professionals tell us that, from a product development standpoint, it's easier to meet a need than it is to create one. If you merge the two concepts, any product or service that results in end users who feel good about themselves ought to be pretty successful. Because customer satisfaction and retention is critical to long-term success, making customers feel important is a key element in the process. Because doing so requires motivated employees (customer service is always a reflection of employee satisfaction) who feel their role is important, you begin to see how important it is to avoid this Mess-Up.

Restoring dignity

When I was a teenager, my father asked me to memorize a poem written by O.S. Marden. While the specific phrases elude me today, its basic message has been a part of my personal philosophy since I first committed it to memory. The message of the poem is that the right of all people to be treated with dignity, regardless of the jobs they perform. One part of the poem reads, "Many a great man has sat at a cobbler's bench or forged at an anvil." It concludes by saying it isn't the job that dignifies the man, but the man who dignifies the job. To me the message was: Treat everyone with respect. Grant no person a larger portion of kindness and attention simply because of his or her station or wealth. This is what making people feel special is all about.

One of the ways we can make both customers and employees feel special is to honor them where they are. Once, a sales rep called me with a small order. "These guys aren't that much," he said. "They need the parts quickly, but I wouldn't bust my butt for them." If a company with a service commitment makes a distinction between who will or will not receive that service based on the size of the order, a crisis of legitimacy with employees will occur. It won't take long for them to figure out that if you're a little guy, you're expendable, and that the same evaluation process might apply to them as well.

Doing it right

I remember touring a company's facilities several years ago and having an opportunity to speak with many of their employees. I was impressed at the confidence each one showed. Everyone seemed to feel that his or her presence in that operation was a key element in its success. The last person I spoke with was a young man who worked in maintenance. When I met him, he was getting ready to cut the grass, which already looked immaculate. "You do a terrific job," I commented, nodding toward the well-manicured landscape. "I have to," he replied. Signaling me to draw closer he said, "Mr. Smith says I have the most important job. He says the customer's first impression is the one he draws when he first sees our plant." I smiled to myself as I left, because this employee was the fifth one to tell me that Mr. Smith, the company's president, thought their job to be most important.

One manager I know makes it a point to acknowledge his staff's efforts both individually and corporately.

If a customer calls or writes to express appreciation for the service rendered by a member of his staff, he calls the department together to read the praise out loud. The praise of the manager is accompanied by the "atta-boys" of his or her coworkers. He doesn't stop there, though. He writes a formal letter on the company's stationery commending the efforts of that employee as specifically as possible. One copy of the letter goes to the individual, another into their personnel file, and one to the president of the company, who makes it a point to walk back and congratulate the worker. Do you think this procedure makes that employee feel important?

The same manager has a similar strategy for customers. He is constantly looking for unique ways to express his appreciation when customers give him business. His favorite method is to send his customers a box containing helium-filled balloons that escape when opened. Inside the box are a bag of candy and a handwritten note of appreciation. Not only does he thank his customer in a special way, he does it in a memorable way. Instead of sending Christmas cards to his customers, he sends Thanksgiving cards. "I want my customers to know I appreciate them and am thankful for their business," he says. The fact that his message doesn't get lost in hundreds of Christmas cards is not lost on him either.

Turning failure into victory

1. Listen! Listen! Listen! As already covered in Mess-Up No. 5, listening is the most powerful and persuasive thing a manager can do. When we listen to other people, we give away our most important and treasured resource— our time. This alone conveys a powerful message.

2. Be gracious. Graciousness means demonstrating kindness and goodwill to another person. It involves courteous consideration of others' interests, as well as a disposition to oblige them (see Mess-Up No. 52).

3. Express appreciation often and in writing. Acknowledging a person's contribution is an obvious (but overlooked) step in reinforcing that person's importance. The Extinction Theory says that any good behavior that goes unacknowledged will eventually disappear. While verbal appreciation is important, written appreciation has real staying power.

4. Invest in employees. Nothing makes staff feel more important than believing they are part of the bigger picture. Demonstrate their importance by investing in their future. When possible, send them to seminars and workshops that help them to increase their skill (and worth).

5. Invest in customers. Look for creative ways to send an age-old message: Thanks! The time spent in making customers aware of their importance and value is one investment that will pay huge dividends.

Mess-Up No. 11

Failure to recognize there is no such thing as "stretch socks" management.

"My idea of an agreeable person is someone who agrees with me."

—Benjamin Disraeli, 19th-century British prime minister

The different personality styles of people never cease to amaze me. I recently met two sisters who vividly illustrate my point. While both share a common enthusiasm for business, the areas that interest each reflect the differences in their personalities. The older woman, a bank auditor, loves detail. She likes to plan, coordinate, and analyze. She is well-organized and always aware of priorities, but flexible enough to handle interruptions and schedule changes when they arise. Although she communicates well with people and has a strong customer focus, she would rather do anything but sell, a job she thinks anyone can do. Not surprisingly, she likes a high degree of structure and order in her life.

The other sister has a degree in retail marketing. She works for a major cosmetics company setting up distributors throughout the United States. Unlike her sister, she loves to sell. She has excellent communication skills, and has a passion for service. She views selling as a professional vocation, and moves through the process with one objective in mind—satisfying customers' needs. She meets people easily, and uses that talent to connect quickly with customers. She likes the competition associated with selling and looks forward to getting the reports each month to see how she compares with other divisions. She's an idea person, able to conceptualize and create.

Hiring the right person for the right job may well be the greatest challenge that managers face. Fortunately for the women previously mentioned, they appear to have jobs that suit their personality styles. If they were to trade positions, however, neither would find the new work as interesting or as motivating as the work she currently does. One of the biggest Mess-Ups managers can make is to assume that all people are basically the same. This "stretch socks" (one-size-fits-all) approach to management frequently results in the wrong person being placed in the wrong position. The result is often a frustrated and demotivated employee.

Assessing personalities

There are many tools available to help managers assess the personality styles of people. They range from simple observation to complex tests and surveys, such as the Myers-Briggs Type Indicator, that must be administered and scored by trained professionals. There are, however, simpler surveys that can be given that provide a "general reading" on the person's attitude, values, and preferences. These tests usually take an hour or less to administer and can be quickly scored. Many are available as software packages that generate a more detailed analysis of the responses given.

If personality surveys are used, either as a preemployment tool or as a benchmarking tool for current employees, care should be taken not to overemphasize the results. In fact, companies that specialize in these reports recommend they contribute to no more than 30 percent of the decision you make with regard to the person surveyed. One-on-one conversation, background checks, educational background, and past experience all contribute to a more complete and reliable assessment of the person's capabilities and interests.

Personality surveys are best used as part of the preemployment process. Although I've never used a survey to exclude an applicant, I have used them effectively to determine the best questions to ask in the job interview. For example, a test given to one applicant being considered for an inside sales position said they were extremely outgoing and needed constant interaction with other people. On the surface, that seems like a good personality trait for someone who has to talk to a lot of customers. For the purpose of the interview, however, it raises another question: Is the person likely to let their need to socialize interfere with his or her work?

And the winner is...

If the tests are administered to the staff after employment has occurred, great care must be taken to assure each person of the purpose. I remember presenting a sales seminar to a group of senior managers at a bank. Because the financial market had strongly favored the bank for several years, most of the staff was better at order-taking than order-getting. Deregulation changed that. With an emphasis being placed by their CEO on the need to hit the streets and drum up new business, everyone was painfully aware of the need to improve sales skills. For most of the managers, the idea of selling was a threatening concept to begin with.

Part of the seminar to be presented included a section on communication skills, and touched briefly on the benefits of identifying the personality style of a prospect. When the bank's vice president noted this section in my outline, she asked if we could conduct personality surveys as a part of the training session itself. I indicated that we could, but that they would be somewhat shallow in terms of the information yielded. She asked that we give them anyway. She also asked that a copy of the results be given to her at the conclusion of the program to be included in each employee's personnel file.

The workshop got off to a great start with lots of energy, enthusiasm, and participation. For six hours, it was one of the best programs I have ever been a part of. After the lunch break, I told the group we were going to talk a little about personality styles. "At the request of the bank," I informed them, "we're going to give a short personality test to everyone and allow each to process his or her own survey." As the tests were being passed out, I heard several jokes exchanged about what kind of style people perceived others to have. "I'd bet the farm," one person said to another, "that you're a socializer!" Everyone laughed.

After the surveys were completed, I led the group through the process of interpreting their answers. The survey I used grouped most people into one of four categories: steady, influencing, dominant, or cautious. Most personality surveys use similar groupings, but have different names. As we were scoring the surveys, I noticed a significant drop in the energy level of the audience. Employees who had been joking around minutes before were now subdued. I later learned that most people thought you needed to be an influencing personality to do well in sales.

When the surveys revealed them to be steady or cautious, they felt their jobs might be in jeopardy. The fact that the surveys were being turned in to management didn't help.

Before you begin

Personality surveys are a valuable tool, but if you're going to use them, there are a couple of guidelines to follow. First, before giving the surveys, assure all who take them that there is no such thing as "best" style. Had I covered this more effectively in my sales workshop, people would have known that all personality types can be effective salespeople. Second, let people know that just because they have a core style in which they are most comfortable, it does not mean they cannot take on the characteristics of other styles when needed. Lastly, tell those taking the tests that a wide variety of styles are needed for a company to function best.

Turning failure into victory

1. Acknowledge the fact that we are all different. Recognize that personality surveys are a useful tool for getting a general feel for another person's style, and are helpful in determining the best way to relate to that individual.
2. Take care to discover the personality style of each employee. This will enable you to not only communicate with each person in the manner best for them, but to develop a general idea of what might be motivating to each as well.
3. Recognize the fact that there is no one best personality style. The best companies are the ones that have a variety of styles offering unique perspectives on opportunities and problems alike.
4. Recognize that although most of us have a core style we are most likely to default to, we are able to move easily in and out of many personality styles.
5. Personality surveys are certainly not infallible, and should be used in conjunction with other pertinent data

to form an overall picture of an employment candidate or a current employee.

Mess-Up No. 12

Failure to understand the power of genuine praise and encouragement.

"It ain't no fun fighting for a man when, no matter what you've done, it ain't good enough."

—Stephen Crane,
The Red Badge of Courage

A number of years ago I boarded a plane in Hartford, Connecticut, and was surprised to see that the gentleman sitting beside me was wearing a beanie inscribed, "Yale, Class of '29." We quickly struck up a conversation and I learned that he had just attended his 65th class reunion at Yale. As we traveled on, I found myself enthralled by this man's tales. How many people have you spoken with who were on the floor of the New York Stock Exchange the day it collapsed? The man was a walking history lesson.

As we got to know each other, I discovered my companion had enjoyed a successful career in finance, rising from a junior clerk in a large Kansas brokerage firm to become president and CEO. Although retired, he had continued to be a student of the market and now, at the age of 87, still served as a part-time consultant. As we flew over Pittsburgh, I asked a question I like to pose to people who have achieved success and prominence in their careers. "What do you know today," I inquired, "that you wish you had known in the beginning?"

Over the years when I've asked this question, I've picked up some pretty interesting advice. With a lifetime spent in the high-powered world of finance, I expected my companion's response to be rooted in that discipline.

He contemplated my question for a moment before responding. "I guess what I wish I had known 50 years ago," he said, "was how much power I had to affect a person's performance by being their encourager." Although the answer surprised me, I thought his advice may have been the most significant I had received in terms of increasing employee performance.

A lack of encouragement can be a debilitating factor in a business. Like the soldier in *The Red Badge of Courage* shocked to receive the criticism of his general after fighting as hard as he could, employees are fed up with managers who fail to acknowledge their efforts. In a meeting I attended several years ago, I heard employers whispering "pull" every time someone had a suggestion. These employees saw their managers as skeet shooters and their ideas as clay pigeons. They were all expecting to get shot down!

Several years ago, I worked with a company that was having significant morale problems. What emerged during a period of one-on-one sessions I had with their employees was a festering resentment toward the president of the company. The man, it seems, had raised discouragement to an art form. If the company had a good month, his word of encouragement would be "better." If it had a poor month, he would imply that people had been goofing off. After one particularly bad month, the man gave employees nicknames that implied a poor effort on their part ("Limping Larry," "Cruisin' Carol," "Snoozing Sam"). "If the best you can hope for is an insult," one of his employees said, "why make the effort?"

In search of an encouraging word

My grandmother was a remarkable woman. A German immigrant, what she lacked in language mastery, she more than overcame with an intimidating presence. It was a standing joke in our family to ask her what she wanted each year for Christmas. "All I vant," she'd say in her heavy accent, "iss a kind vurd." If the truth were known, she was expecting big stuff just like the rest of us! The truth is that there are many people who would be glad to trade all they receive at Christmas for one kind word. The art of encouragement—and it is indeed that—is one that few managers seem to possess. I remember a participant in a seminar recently telling me he would willingly give up a raise for an occasional pat on the back. He was not exaggerating.

Many managers excuse themselves in this area by saying that the ability to encourage is a gift. I remember giving a president some feedback from a meeting I had with his staff. "The group," I told him, "is hungry for some recognition and encouragement from you." "I'd like to do it," he said, "but it's not a style I'm comfortable with. I think," he added, "it's just something you're born with." Nothing could be further from the truth. Every encourager is the product of another. In an environment where praise and encouragement flow freely, all will learn to give praise and encouragement. As a manager, it will be your responsibility to create this kind of work environment for yourself and for your employees.

Getting the orange slip

When I was younger, I had an opportunity to work for a man who understood the power of encouragement. He was a demanding man, who required maximum effort from his employees. If you did not do what was expected, you could expect to receive his immediate and forceful feedback. If you did perform, however, you would receive his quick and sincere appreciation. That appreciation frequently came in the form of a note written on orange paper, his private stock. His words and punctuation would always be exaggerated ("Awwww Right!!!") for extra effect. These messages of encouragement were so highly valued that employees would run to their desks if they saw an orange note in their in-basket. The criticism could be rough, but you accepted the bad with the good because it was fair.

To receive encouragement, you must first offer encouragement. When you make others feel good about themselves, they in turn will feel good about you and learn to express it. You might call it a law of reciprocity. To some, this may sound like a mutual admiration society. It isn't. Admiration can be given from a distance. Encouragement has to be delivered up close and personal. If you want real power in an organization, master the art of encouragement. The result will be employees who feel valued and who are willing to give their time and creative energy to advance the cause of their employer.

Turning failure into victory

1. Take care to avoid a crisis of legitimacy by using encouragement as a tool to get something done. True encouragement, encouragement that raises confidence and self-esteem, comes without strings attached.

2. Encourage others when it is genuinely deserved. By taking care to select the action to be reinforced, you can avoid the negative effects of unmerited praise.

3. Don't lose sight of the need to encourage. It's easy to get distracted by the daily problems and challenges and to forget the needs of those you work with. Providing encouragement is as important as the other functions of management.

4. Look for creative ways to convey your message, but don't overlook the power of a written note. In a business world dominated by e-mail, a handwritten message has real impact.

5. Encourage superiors, too. Some may feel it inappropriate, but even the boss needs to hear a kind word occasionally. Besides, seldom will a person be the recipient of kind words without looking for a way to return the favor.

Mess-Up No. 13

Failure to understand that motivation is an inner drive, not something we can do to one another.

"Even God cannot talk to a hungry man except in terms of bread."

—Mohandas K. Gandhi,
Indian religious and political leader

The approach to Kentucky State Reformatory in LaGrange is formidable. To gain entry, visitors must process through several checkpoints before gaining access to the massive front gate. Just inside the main door, outsiders must pass through a dual gate security system. For a brief moment, when the heavy iron gate in the rear thuds closed and the one in front remains locked, visitors get an authentic taste of what inmates experience 24 hours a day. It was at this point, when I stood trapped between the gates, that I began to consider the wisdom of my decision to bring knowledge to the residents of Kentucky's largest prison.

When the gate in front of me finally opened, I wasted no time exiting and walking quickly to the door leading to the prison yard. I felt a sigh of relief as I stepped out into the warm afternoon sunshine. My misgivings seemed to fade as I started across a courtyard the size of several football fields. The only thing between me and the concrete building containing my classroom were a few prisoners picking up litter. As I walked across the quadrangle, however, I was startled by a chorus of catcalls, jeers, and "invitations" from bored prisoners in the surrounding buildings. Whatever delusions I had held earlier about making a difference in the penal system were rapidly disappearing.

I learned a lot about motivation that spring in Kentucky. When I was asked to teach a course in business law at the prison, I saw it as an opportunity to make a contribution to society. Besides, I was a little curious about life in a prison and those who reside there. Perhaps it was that curiosity that led me to invite each of the students in my class the first day to stand and share a little about themselves. I learned that day that when you ask a prisoner to share his background, he will invariably include the reason for his incarceration. The reasons given ranged from forgery to manslaughter. Eleven of the group—exactly half—had taken another person's life. Despite this wake-up call, I was encouraged by the friendliness of the group and what I perceived to be an enthusiasm for learning.

Over a period of six weeks, we thoroughly covered the material leading to the first testing period. On the day of the test, I asked each of my students to make sure there was at least one empty chair between them and the next person. They dutifully spread out around the room. One prisoner took great pains to isolate himself in a corner. I explained the test procedure and informed everyone I would be watching them to make sure all eyes remained on their own papers. I distributed the tests and assumed a warden-like position at the head of the class. I checked my watch, and then instructed them to begin.

About 15 minutes into the test, one of the inmates—a fellow named Keith—called across the room to a friend: "Hey Eric, what did you get for number four?" "C," Eric responded. "Thanks, man," Keith replied. Before I could recover from my surprise, another inmate called out to no one in particular: "Did anyone get the answer to number 12?" "Chattel," the response came from the rear of the class. I quickly called a halt to the test and informed everyone that if these outbursts continued, it would result in a failed grade for the entire class. "Whatta ya gonna do," one of the inmates asked, "put us in jail?"

The myths of motivation

Why people do the things they do is one of the least understood areas of human behavior. Theories abound, but real understanding is in short supply. Every day managers make decisions based on commonly accepted misconceptions in hopes of increasing performance. The effects are frequently demotivating, as I learned at the prison. Here are a few of the more common myths of motivation.

Myth No. 1: Motivation is something we can do *to* each other. Motivation, by definition, is an inner drive. It's something inside a person that moves them toward goals that satisfy particular needs. Suppose, for example, a person is broke and has gone without eating for a couple of days. He comes to you and offers to work for food. You tell him that if he will clean your garage, you will buy him a Big Mac. The tendency here is to believe you're motivating this man to work by offering food. In reality, if the hunger, his inner drive, were not present, he would not do the work. It's his hunger, not your Big Mac, which is the motivating factor in his decision to work.

Myth No. 2: Some people are just not motivated. Everyone is motivated, just not by the same things. The secret to good management lies in discovering each employee's unmet needs and looking for ways to fulfill them. Let me illustrate. A number of years ago I purchased a new computer which included a number of educational tools and databases. I sat down with my then teenage daughter and demonstrated each to her, making a reasoned pitch for the value of computer literacy. Despite my best selling efforts, she appeared to have little interest.

Several days later, my wife and I informed her that we had decided to go ahead and buy her a car now instead of waiting several months until she began her college commute. She was ecstatic. When I came home that evening, she presented me with a printout of prices and buying tips on the model we had discussed. "Where did you get this?" I asked. "Off the computer," she answered. "Where on the computer?" I countered. "Oh," she responded, "there's all kinds of good stuff on the Internet." What I wanted to occur in my daughter's life—computer literacy—had happened. But for her reasons, not mine.

Myth No. 3: The most common motivator in business is money. Many managers assume that, if enough money is involved, employees will do anything—and like it! I remember talking with a manager who was complaining about a good employee who had left to accept another position. "I can't believe it," he exclaimed, "he actually left for a job that paid *less* money!" I couldn't sympathize with this manager, because I had once done the same thing.

I was just out of college and had secured a position as a customer service supervisor for a local company. Wanting to do well on my first real job, I enthusiastically undertook every assignment. Each task was done well and on time. Over a period of several years, I received a number of raises. Each, however, was presented as if a gift from my manager. He would call me into his office and say, "Well, I managed to scrounge up some money for you." No link was ever made between my performance and the increase. My manager thought the money alone would keep me motivated, but the exact opposite occurred. My inner drive craved recognition for a job well-done. The money was nice, but it wasn't enough.

In a post 9/11 world where employees are reevaluating the reasons they work and what they want from a job (jobs with meaning and purpose now top the list), a greater understanding of the nature of personal motivation is essential.

Turning failure into victory

1. When it comes to motivation, the one-size-fits-all approach is out. Take time to discover the unique needs of each of your employees. Give them realistic feedback on the chances of fulfilling those needs in their present jobs. Honesty can be highly motivating, too.

2. Once you've discovered what your employees want and need, create opportunities for them to achieve it. Let them know that a significant portion of your responsibility is making sure their jobs are personally satisfying.

3. Understand that motivation is more about emotion than logic. Don't get hung up on your perceptions of what makes sense. If an employee seems more motivated by recognition than money, don't let your view of his or her choice keep you from addressing that need.

4. Remember that satisfied needs are not motivators. If something that once seemed to motivate an employee no longer does, go back to the beginning and find a new, unfulfilled need. Rest assured that one does exist.

5. Remember that praise, recognition, information, respect, time off, meaningful work, high visibility, performance reviews, and access to top management may exceed money as motivating factors in a person's work. None of these, however, should be offered in place of money.

Part 4:
Managing Change

Mess-Up No. 14

Failure to solicit input from employees before making changes that affect their responsibilities.

"Once you decide to make a change in a particular area, it often means a change in people, and that's most often where things bog down."

—Q.T. Wiles, turnaround operations consultant

Cabin fever can be disruptive, especially if the inhabitants of the cabin are all members of the same department. Several years ago, a group of workers I managed were struggling through a long and challenging winter. Quite frankly, we were getting on each other's nerves and it was showing in our performance. Sales were down, complaints were up, and there was no end in sight. No matter how you measured it, we just weren't getting the job done. It was a classic case of winter blahs. After some thought, I decided to break the fever by giving the cabin (office) a new look. Although excited by my idea, I decided to keep it secret until the change had been completed.

One weekend, without letting anyone know, I completely rearranged the office. Every desk, table and chair was given a new home; every filing cabinet and potted plant a new location. I labored diligently for several hours until I had everything just right. I smiled as I left that weekend, anticipating the comments—effusive praise?—that would surely flow in my direction on Monday. I could just hear everyone gushing in unison about how insightful and wonderful I was as a manager.

On Monday morning I arrived early so I could see everyone's reaction as the effect of my management genius first struck. Big mistake! The first person to arrive said nothing, but her silence spoke volumes. When the others arrived, the reaction was one of collective dismay. Instead of praise, I received condemnation. I tried my best to convince everyone that the new look would breathe fresh life and energy into the department if they'd only give it a chance. Nothing doing. The grumbling continued all week long, accompanied by a further reduction in productivity.

By the end of the week, I was ready to throw in the towel. My little experiment in "change therapy" had failed miserably. I called everyone together on Friday afternoon and promised that on Monday morning, everything would be back in its original location. My announcement was greeted by a chorus of cheers. "Thank goodness he's regained his senses," I overheard one of my charges mutter. "Yeah," another said, "I thought he'd lost it there for a while."

Another long weekend of moving furniture rectified my error. With everything back in its original place, everyone seemed happy again. Everyone, that was, but me. I still felt something was needed to break out of our rut. Halfway through the week, I called everyone together and shared my feelings. I informed them that I thought some changes were needed, that our productivity was down, and that we had become complacent. I told them I had thought a new look might breathe some life back into the group, but obviously it hadn't. I decided to give them ownership of the situation. "Give me your ideas on solving this problem," I requested.

Around noon, a couple of the staff members came into my office and said, "We've been talking it over and we think you're right. A new look just might shake things up." We agreed that the department would accept responsibility for what those changes would look like. Later in the day I noticed a layout of the office, complete with cutouts for desks and chairs had been taped to the wall. Several people were busy negotiating where each wanted to be in the new arrangement.

For the rest of the week I observed a high level of animation as everyone shifted and positioned the paper cutouts that represented their space. By the end of the week, I received unanimous approval on the new office layout. I told employees that when they returned to work the following Monday, the office would be changed to reflect the layout they had chosen. Everyone seemed excited about the pending changes. Several workers offered to come in over the weekend and help with the move.

On Monday, the new layout was greeted with smiles and laughter. The revised look seemed to breathe enthusiasm and energy into our department, and our productivity rose immediately. One of our sales reps, calling the office to check on a delivery commented about how upbeat everyone seemed. Indeed they were.

Everything we had hoped to achieve had been accomplished. It was ironic that the layout chosen by our group, with the exception of a filing cabinet or two, was the same one so roundly rejected several weeks before. The second office revision was greeted with cheers instead of jeers because those responsible for carrying out the change were involved in its creation.

The mystery of change

Change is a curious thing. Some people absolutely thrive on it. But for most, a less-than-perfect reality is more comfortable than an unknown possibility. The successful implementation and acceptance of change are dependent on the degree to which a manager prepares his or her group to be "change masters." The manager who encourages flexibility and responsiveness, who fosters creativity and risk-taking, who challenges his group to take ownership of the problems they face will have gone a long way in preparing his team for an unpredictable future.

Turning failure into victory

1. Avoid surprises. For change to be responded to in positive fashion, good communication is essential. Define the reason for the change upfront, then give people updates each step along the way. Communicate early, communicate often.

2. To secure commitment to proposed changes, make sure the people implementing the change have a voice. While communication is important, so is participation. Get everyone involved at some level in the process. Use as many of their ideas as you can, and fully explain the ones you cannot.

3. Convey the benefits of proposed changes for every individual. Unless those responsible for carrying out the change will benefit from it, little will get done. Give people legitimate reasons for implementing the changes you make.

4. Give people control over some portion of the changes being implemented. It's important for employees to feel they have some degree of influence over their future.

5. Be a change champion, but be sure to carry out your own responsibilities in making change work. Don't be like the juggler who tossed his balls in the air, then expected someone else to run under and catch them. Remember the key ingredients of managing change: define, inform, discuss, update.

Mess-Up No. 15

Failure to understand why people resist change.

"They could not bring themselves at the moment of crisis to surrender their memories and alter the antique patterns of their lives."

—J.H. Elliott, historian on Imperial Spain

"We need help," the head of human resources said. "We're trying to install new scheduling software, and everybody is very upset about it." "I know it's a difficult change to make," I said, recalling my own bad experiences with a similar system change. I tried to encourage her by telling her what I had been told at the time. "Changing information systems is a lot like potty training your kid," I said. "It's pretty messy at the beginning, but it does get better." The wisdom of my humor escaping her, she replied, "Well, right now we've got a lot of people who feel like they're stuck holding the dirty diaper."

As we discussed her situation further, I learned that the degree of anger and alienation felt by her staff was unusually severe. "Unfortunately," she said, "our management team is not the most tolerant in the world. I think part of their problem is that they're responsible for implementing a program they had little input on. They feel like they're stuck trying to defend something they aren't convinced is necessary in the first place." She went on to say that many of the managers were giving less than total support. Some were impeding its progress by deliberately dragging their feet.

My assignment was to talk to staff members about their frustrations, then present a program to the management team on implementing change. My interviews with staff members were interesting, to say the least. I knew that people often resist change, but I wasn't prepared for the emotional intensity that accompanied that resistance. One woman, a customer service representative whose whole method of entering orders had been revised, was on the verge of tears. "Nothing works right," she said. "I have a customer on the phone screaming at me because his order is late, and I can't even access that screen anymore to get an answer. How am I supposed to get anything accomplished this way?"

Out in production, the situation wasn't much better. The plant manager was furious when I entered his office because his material status report—his daily bible when it comes to shipping orders—wasn't available due to a system glitch. When I asked the man if he had any suggestions on what to do with the system, his response was less than complimentary. I realized at this point that the company's attitude toward the new system bordered on anarchy.

Expect resistance

Leading others through periods of change is one of the most important tasks managers handle. How well they accomplish this may well determine the future success of both the organization and the manager executing the responsibility. The harsh reality of life—in both a business and personal sense—is that most people view change as something to be avoided at all cost. Robert Kennedy once said, "Progress is a nice word, but change is its motivator. And change has its enemies." Kennedy's tragic death may be evidence of the extremes to which people can go to avoid change.

Understanding why people resist change is essential to the successful execution of a change strategy. While the reasons for resistance are varied in both content and intensity, certain rationales of resistance seem to rank at or near the top. Here's a closer look at six of the more significant ones.

1. **Change is just another chance to fail.** Although not a productive activity, it's our nature to be fearful. Someone once described fear as picturing life the way

you don't want it to be, vividly and with imagination! Many fears are associated with change. A few fears that come to mind include a fear of embarrassment, a fear of uncertainty, a fear of being misunderstood, a fear of being left behind, a fear of disappointment, and a fear of losing ground. All of these can be lumped together into one broad category—a fear of failure. Throughout our lives we are conditioned to believe that failure is the worst thing that can happen to a person. As a result, we spend much of our lives in a cautious attempt to minimize the chances of that occurring. That strategy does not include risking change.

2. I've already won. I remember once trying to implement a new procedure in my department. I encountered considerable resistance from one of my staff, a man who had been with the company longer than me, who told me there was no way he was going to go along with the new program. At first, I assumed the conflict was a seniority issue. Because I was new to the company, I thought that maybe he felt he had a better handle on what was going on than I did. The real reason for his resistance, I learned in a later discussion, was a more practical one. "Had I gone along with your proposal," he said, "things for me personally would have gotten worse." Believing he had already won, he saw no benefit in changing.

3. Cynicism. In his book *The Dilbert Principle*, Scott Adams offers an interesting perspective of change and change management. Adams writes:

"The goal of change management is to dupe slow-witted employees into thinking change is good for them by appealing to their sense of adventure and love of challenge. This is like convincing a trout to leap out of a stream to experience the adventure of getting deboned."

One of the main reasons for the outrageous success of Dilbert is the high level of cynicism that exists in business today. Companies all across America are staffed by employees who feel disillusioned, disheartened, and expendable. Many people today resist change because of the lack of trust they have in the motives of their employers and managers.

4. A love affair with existing tools. Many people develop a sense of self-worth and value based on the expertise they have with existing tools. When changes come along that suggest another tool (process, program, procedure) be used, resistance based on a fear of obsolescence occurs. I know a woman who went to work for a company a number of years ago and brought along a software program she liked to use for desktop publishing. Her manager told her that the company preferred another program, one already available on the company's network. She resisted the change. She was comfortable with her present program and felt it was best for the work she did. It became a source of friction between her and her boss, eventually resolved by her premature departure. There are some battles that are not in your best interest to win.

5. Unresolved prior experience. For many people, past experiences with change have not been happy ones. For these people, change raises a whole specter of negative feelings, such as rejection, disappointment, displacement, uncertainty, or even obsolescence. Because these prior feelings were never resolved, they tend to be projected on any attempt to implement change. Unless these concerns are surfaced, listened to, and honored, the chances for moving forward together are compromised.

6. Loss of control. My wife doesn't appreciate my Formula One driving skills. When I head into a curve, I love to downshift and stretch the car's cornering capability to the max. During these fits of driving exuberance, my wife usually complains that I'm bouncing her around the car. "I didn't think it was all that bad," I say. "Well," she invariably replies, "you have the advantage of holding onto the wheel and knowing in advance what you're going to do." It occurred to me recently that my wife has pinpointed one of the primary reasons people resist change: loss of control (see Mess-Up No. 34). Management often fails to feel the turbulence associated with change because they have their hands on the wheel and know in advance where they plan to go. Those adjusting to the change usually feel like they're getting bounced all over the place.

Securing employee support

Getting employees to support change requires an awareness of the wide array of reasons why people resist it, and a plan for dealing with those objections. The manager who implements change well is the one most adept at helping his team get comfortable with uncertainty.

Turning failure into victory

1. Teach your group the disadvantages—both personal and corporate—of becoming root-bound. Encourage people to become flexible problem-solvers and calculated risk takers by walking them through hypothetical change scenarios before they are needed.

2. Nearly 90 percent of the decisions one makes daily are fully programmed. Help your employees to realize how much past experiences effect individual perceptions of reality. Encourage them to overcome biases regarding change.

3. Encourage your staff to develop a whole-world vision. Employees need to see themselves as part of a system, not just another cog in the wheel. Get them out of their comfort zones by giving them tasks outside their normal responsibilities.

4. Apply the "shared knowledge" concept. Whenever possible, keep information in motion and available to all. One major reason employees resist change is the surprise element. Keep them informed to minimize resistance.

5. Increase trust by increasing listening opportunities during periods of proposed change. Employees who are

allowed to give input are more willing to give their managers the benefit of the doubt in supporting change.

◻

Mess-Up No. 16

Failure to understand and manage the mechanics of change.

"One thing that is new is the prevalence of newness, the changing scale and scope of change itself, so that the world alters as we walk in it."

—J. Robert Oppenheimer, physicist and director of the Manhattan Project

Winston Churchill once wrote that to improve was to change. "To be perfect," he said, "is to change often." Change is certainly not a new concept. Confucius, Heraclitus, and Plato made it a popular topic of discussion years before the birth of Christ. While change itself is nothing new, the speed and frequency of that change certainly is. I heard a comment recently that our world is changing so fast that printed information is considered obsolete simply because it was old enough to have been through the U.S. mail!

Today's businessperson must accept the fact that life in the future will be lived out in a state of constant change. Today's managers, more than ever before, need to understand the mechanics of change, and how to lead their employees through a potential minefield of uncertainty. Helping employees to anticipate and understand the changes that will most certainly come will be one of the major responsibilities of management in the 21st century. For managers to carry out this responsibility, they must be able to understand, anticipate, and direct change.

The mechanics of change

Implementing change successfully requires managers who understand how change works. Many do not, and they spend a great portion of their time trying to cope with the people problems it creates. To understand change, it's best to "raise the hood" and see what makes it run. Change, in the sense we're discussing it, is the planned or unplanned response of an organization or individual to internal or external pressures. Despite its uncertainty, there are a few things we can say about change with a degree of confidence. We know, for example, that it's an ongoing process, that it's progressive (it builds upon itself), that it initiates movement that forces decisions and that those decisions have consequences.

Ironically, if you don't like change, you really have to blame yourself. Most of the changes that are taking place in business are initiated by consumers who demand the latest and greatest of everything. We want products and services that are fast, cheap, abundant, and of good quality. Oh, yeah, we want lots of choices, too. Not surprisingly, some of the principal driving forces of change include speed, convenience, choices, value, customer service, and quality. To identify potential sources of change, all a manager has to do is look at these categories and ask, "How does my company respond?" The areas of deficiency are where most changes are likely to occur.

According to research, all change has its own unique pattern. Components of that pattern include the direction it's taking, its magnitude, its frequency, its duration, its impact, and its speed. Change is often like looking at a complex tapestry from the wrong side. Very little is discernible. By understanding the components of a change pattern, however, the effect is like flipping that tapestry over and seeing the logic of its design.

Structural vs. cyclical change

Structural change represents a fundamental transformation from some previous state. Typically, structural change begins slowly, accelerates rapidly, levels off, and is generally permanent. Business consultant and author Leon Martel says that structural change often requires dismantling old institutions, relationships, and procedures and replacing them with entirely new ones. "We cannot expect," he writes, "to move into the future with the baggage of the past."

Cyclical change is temporary change that generally does not cause permanent alterations in the structure of an organization. Some characteristics of cyclical change include repetition, limited duration, and a high likelihood of reversal. The key characteristic of cyclical change is that it is temporary. Companies need to take care not to over-invest in cyclical change. Responses to this type of change must be the kind that can be easily reversed in the future.

Common errors

Managers faced with leading their organizations through the perilous waters of constant change need to take care to avoid a few common pitfalls. The first is believing that the ideas and concepts used to solve yesterday's problems will be sufficient for the future. Companies forced to constantly reinvent themselves need new ideas and new direction. The second pitfall to avoid is believing that current trends will continue. It's important to determine if the change to which you're responding is structural or cyclical. The last pitfall to avoid is that of neglecting the opportunities that change presents. Companies that try to avoid change may find that their competitors have passed them by.

Turning failure into victory

1. The best way to prepare for change is to understand it. Take time to analyze the changes before you in terms of their type (structural or cyclical), pattern, and relevance to your organization.

2. Effective change management requires managers with an idea of where the next changes may be coming from.

Make information-gathering a constant part of your job. I know one manager who scans magazine and newspaper headlines at the airport to track emerging trends.

3. Teach employees to appreciate the possibility of change and to be comfortable with the uncertainty it creates. Keep them involved in the planning and development of any change strategy you create.

4. Encourage employees to accept responsibility for identifying possible changes in their areas of responsibility. One of the best ways to get employee support for future change is to teach them to initiate it.

5. Recognize that change, although unsettling at times, carries with it seeds of prosperity. The Chinese word for crisis is composed of two characters—one representing danger, the other opportunity. Talk to your employees in terms of both.

Mess-Up No. 17

Failure to anticipate change.

"Change can come with breathtaking speed, leaving a company on the defensive and in financial trouble when it's forced to catch up."

—Gary Goldstick and George Schreiber,
Inc. Magazine Guide to Small
Business Success

Alvin Tofler, futurist and author of three seminal books on change (*Future Shock*, *The Third Wave*, and *Power Shift*), says change occurs whenever the future invades the present. My future was never more invaded than in the early morning hours of November 15, 1986, while I was staying at the Asia World Hotel in Taipei, Taiwan. I was roused from my sleep by an annoying vibration that swiftly grew into a window-rattling, plaster-cracking rumble. Half-asleep and totally disoriented, I stumbled to the window and discovered I was in the midst of an earthquake. A big earthquake (6.8 on the Richter scale).

As I stood at the window, one thought drove itself into the center of my consciousness—what the heck does one do in an earthquake? I later discovered instructions conveniently printed on the back of my door, but at the moment I found myself ill-equipped to deal with the situation. A Midwesterner from the States, I had been taught how to deal with tornadoes. Neither of the two pieces of advice that came rushing to mind—"run for the basement" and "always keep fresh batteries handy"—seemed suited to the situation. There I stood, a man prepared for tornadoes, riding out an earthquake. It was a moment characterized by high anxiety, great uncertainty and a significant lack of response on my part.

Winds of change?

Whenever I'm speaking or writing on the subject of change, I find I draw heavily on my earthquake experience. In many respects, the principle challenges faced in business today are earthquakes, too—changes every bit as unsettling and trying as those that occur in nature. A glance backwards reveals a landscape dramatically altered by the events of the recent past. Winds of change that slowly erode the terrain seem to be a thing of the past, and earthquakes seem to be more of a constant than a surprise.

Twenty years ago, we were marveling at the collapse of the Soviet Union and the rise of something called the Internet. When Bill Clinton took the oath of office as President, the primary user of e-mail was the government. Yet, these changes pale in comparison to what business has had to address over the past five years. Unimaginable acts of terrorism have changed how we think and what we value. Mind numbing acts of greed have increased investor cynicism and employee mistrust. PDAs and laptops armed with Bluetooth technology have put a new metric on communication. Last year alone we sent 7 trillion e-mails worldwide.

Acquiring the tools needed to manage people and events in a rapidly changing world requires new ideas, concepts, and skills. Failure to understand the dynamics of change, as well as the mechanics of appropriate response, can have serious consequences. Managers aspiring to become change agents—leaders adept at initiating, managing, and mastering change—need a new set of skills in their repertoire. To become change champions as they wade into the 21st century, managers must first get familiar with the principle stages of change management: anticipation, identification, and implementation.

Anticipating the future

The first, and perhaps most critical, stage of change management is that of anticipation. To maximize opportunity while minimizing risk, managers must develop the capacity to work in the present while keeping an eye firmly on the horizon. I call this the "Stealth Principle." Pilots of these subsonic jets are taught from the beginning that thinking too much in the present can be fatal. At speeds of more than 600 miles per hour, the future becomes the present pretty quickly! To enhance their capacity to anticipate future events, managers must cultivate methods for tracking the future. Four elements assist the manager in this task.

1. **Relentless preparation.** The first element is a commitment to what the Japanese call "kaizen"—continual improvement. In the Japanese culture, kaizen is a philosophical commitment to what I call "forever learning." It's a belief that life is a journey, and that knowledge can and should increase with every step taken. Fail to learn each day, and you give away a portion of your future.

2. Long distance vision. The second element is future-focus, the ability to operate in the present with an eye on the future. Successful change agents must spend a minimum of 25 percent of their time on future-focused issues to avoid being blindsided by market shifts. An excellent example of failing to anticipate change is the Swiss watch industry. In the late 60s it held 90 percent of the available market. Failing to recognize the threat posed by the digital watch, a technology it had discovered and discarded, their market share shriveled to less than 20 percent by 1980.

3. Networking. The third element of good anticipation is connecting with key people. I like the use of the word "connect" instead of communicate. For me, it paints a mental picture of two railroad cars coming together. When the couplers engage, the identity of neither is altered. Yet, they now have the power of two instead of one. Developing a network of key people and staying in touch with them ensures a steady flow of information that will provide a window on future needs.

4. Information gathering. The fourth element of good anticipation is staying informed. Many feel that with the Internet and other interactive media, we're better informed today than ever before. Studies indicate, however, that the vast majority of managers are not keeping themselves up-to-date on the events shaping the future of business. Joel Barker suggests a simple test to see how we're doing. For two months keep track of all information you read, watch, or otherwise access. Then ask yourself, "Is this the material of a future-focused manager?" If the answer is no, you're not anticipating the future.

Turning failure into victory

1. Make the anticipation of change a part of both the long- and short-term planning process. Ask yourself at least once a month what "earthquakes" might alter the landscape of your business. Ask yourself what advantages or benefits each might create.

2. Know in advance what the procedures are for an unexpected change. Make sure your staff knows as well. There's a considerable amount of confidence that comes from knowing a plan exists for dealing with the unknown. (I would have felt much better had I read in advance the directions on the back of my hotel room door.)

3. Make looking ahead a part of your ongoing activities. Nothing is more disconcerting to employees than to see their manager panic in the face of the unexpected.

4. Accept the fact that change is inevitable, and will continue to be throughout our lifetime. The only thing unknown at this point is its speed and frequency. Those who can get comfortable with the certainty of uncertainty will be the ones most likely to profit from it.

5. Keep yourself informed on the events and people that initiate change. Cultivate the reading and viewing habits of a future-focused manager. Keep your network active, current, and filled with people looking to the future. Anticipate the future and be a change leader!

Part 5:
Personal Development

Mess-Up No. 18

Failure to incorporate yourself.

"You are the first product, so positioning yourself in the market as an individual is extremely important."

— Portia Isaacson, founder
and president of Dream It

Thomas Friedman, author of *The World Is Flat: A Brief History of the Twenty-First Century*, had an interesting observation recently. He was asked by an interviewer how things had changed in China over the years. Friedman's response was that in the 50s parents told their kids, "Eat all your food, children in China are starving." Today, he says, they should be telling them, "Do your homework, children in China want your job."

An old, new reality

The nature of business is changing and the impact of these changes is being felt by managers everywhere. According to futurist Alvin Tofler, more than 2,000 jobs are lost in the United States every day. Many of these are management positions. While new jobs are being created to take their place, the fact remains that the American workplace is changing. As more and more companies downsize, restructure, and reengineer, the security of management grows more uncertain.

How do you survive in this atmosphere of rapid change and uncertainty? The answer may lie in the simple process of changing how you view yourself in relation to your company. You may want to consider yourself not as an employee, but as an independent contractor selling your services for a fee. Think of yourself as...*You, Inc.*

Create You, Inc.

Becoming You, Inc. involves changing the perception you have of yourself in relation to your employer. By no means does this imply that you are no longer loyal to your company, or that you are not a team player. It just means that you are now in business for yourself and must change your relationship accordingly. You must do what all businesses do—write a mission statement, select a board of advisors, develop an operating budget, put together a viable product (you), market the product (you again), and take care of your customer (your employer).

You do what?

I had just concluded a frenzied sales pitch to the president of a company who now sat turning my business card over and over in his hands. My startup was only a few months old and, frankly, I was getting a bit anxious to make things happen. In what could only be described as a shotgun blast, I had just given this man more information than he needed, and certainly more than he wanted. Sliding my card back across the desk to me he said, "When you can write what you do on the back of this card, come see me again."

Getting You, Inc. off the ground

Every successful business starts with a good idea of what its purpose is. Incorporating yourself requires putting together a personal mission statement that defines the product or service you will offer to your employer. Like regular mission statements, it should be short and should define your unique "selling points." Here's a sample of a mission statement written by a customer service supervisor in one of our training sessions:

Personal Mission Statement

To provide high-quality customer service that produces noticeable results, such as increased customer loyalty (repeat business), while achieving a sense of personal satisfaction and accomplishment. I will achieve this through:

❖ *My ability to manage time and set priorities.*

❖ *My ability to expeditiously solve a problem.*

❖ *My ability to maintain a professional attitude when difficulties arise.*

❖ *A strong personal work ethic.*

❖ *A strong desire to learn and grow.*

As you can see, this person has a pretty good idea of what business she was in and the "product" she expects to sell to her employer. If you do not have a clear vision of your mission and purpose with your present employer, there's a pretty good chance they won't either.

After your mission statement is complete, your next objective is to establish an operating budget. In other words, how much will you need to spend to keep your product viable? At a time when many companies are cutting back on training and development, you cannot afford the mistake of letting these areas slide. When you become You, Inc., you accept complete responsibility for making sure your product (you) remains current and in line with the needs of your customer (employer). This is where you can develop a real competitive advantage.

Selling the product means letting the buyer know what you have to offer. Again, the focus can be present (what you have to offer now) or future (what you expect to provide over the long haul). Self-promotion is an area in which most people have difficulty, so let me recommend two books. The first is *The Brand You 50* by Tom Peters and the other is *How to Work a Room* by Susan RoAne. These books have been out for a few years, but do an excellent job of teaching you to successfully present yourself to others.

It's not unthinkable that the workplace of the future may be one without employees. Instead, it may be filled with millions of "sole proprietors" selling products and services to customers. Since many companies no longer feel a sense of responsibility for the growth and development of your career, your future is now firmly in your hands and no one else's. As one of my seminar attendees put it, "We're all in this alone!" If you want to thrive, not just survive, in the workplace of the future, take charge (ownership) of your career now.

Turning failure into victory

1. Identify your USF (unique selling factor). Pull out your business card and write on the back (fifteen words or less) what sets you apart from others. Read it over and over until repeating it becomes second nature.

2. Protect your brand. Accept the fact that your employer may feel little responsibility for the growth of your career. Don't take it personal, it's the reality of business. Look for ways to grow your "business" (career) by increasing your value through education, new skills, and experience.

3. It's not disloyal to think of yourself first. This doesn't imply that the decisions you make will be to the detriment of your employer. Quite the contrary. Your reason

for existence as a business is to provide value and to satisfy your customer (employer). Who wouldn't be happy with that arrangement?

4. Always be prepared to find a new customer (employer). This is the reality of being in business for yourself. Any responsible and successful business understands the vagaries of the marketplace. Things change, and you should be ready to do so as well.

5. Ask yourself, "If I invoiced my employer today for services rendered, would they willingly pay the bill?" Remember at all times that staying in business is contingent on the value the business provides.

Mess-Up No. 19

Failure to "scrape the barnacles" by conducting frequent self-appraisals and making the needed adjustments.

"The greatest revolution in our generation is that of human beings, who, by changing the inner attitudes of their minds, can change the outer aspects of their lives."

—Marilyn Ferguson, author

Whenever business takes me to Ireland, I like to stay in a town outside Dublin called Dún Laoghaire. It's a harbor town, and early morning walks along the pier are a personal favorite. I was out one morning and had just passed a Martello Tower used as a home by James Joyce, when I came upon several men vigorously scraping the bottom of a boat. I struck up a conversation with one of the men (an easy thing to do in Ireland), and soon learned that the object of their efforts were little calcified deposits called barnacles. Barnacles are crustaceans that attach themselves to boat bottoms for the equivalent of a free ride.

As we chatted, the man explained to me that the barnacles robbed his vessel of much-needed maneuverability, while reducing overall speed by as much as half. He said his fuel costs rose by a similar amount. To prevent this expense, it is necessary to haul the boat out of the water several times a year to inspect for barnacles. "The little buggers get on a little at a time," he told me, "so you've got to be watching for 'em constantly. They'll steal your speed," he concluded.

The deception of the gradual

My conversation with the fisherman in Ireland reminded me of something I like to call the deception of the gradual. The idea is that most things that work against us in our careers are developed gradually, often deceiving us of their presence. Let me give you a good illustration of what I'm talking about. I attended a trade show in Paris once with the objective of gathering as much competitive information as possible. Over a period of several days, I filled a bag with catalogs and literature, hauling it to my hotel room twice daily. As individual loads, I didn't notice the weight that much. When I put everything into my suitcase for the return trip, I noticed that my load had increased dramatically.

When I reached Orly International for the return flight to the States, I had difficulty just getting the bag on the scales. It was really packed! After weighing my bags, the ticket agent informed me that I was over the weight limit and would have to pay a considerable surcharge. I told her I would think about it, and then hauled my baggage to a nearby trash receptacle. I began going through my stuff, deciding what I was willing to pay for and what I was not. I had soon discarded much of what I had collected, and returned home without having to pay a penalty.

Life is like that. We cruise along, often unaware of the wide variety of barnacle-like habits that attach themselves to us. Like the boats in Dun Laighaire Harbor, the result is a loss of the maneuverability needed to survive in a world that places a premium on being fast, flexible, and fluid. To succeed in a hyper-competitive environment that seems to change daily, we need to periodically scrape away the stuff slowing us down.

Personal barnacles

What is slowing you down? What traditions, habits, or mind-sets are causing you to be left behind in the Great Management Race? In my seminars, this question is put to participants who are given time to do a little soul searching on the topic. Here's a list of some of the "barnacles" that have been identified over the years:

- Perfectionism.
- Disorganization.
- Fear of change.
- Fear of responsibility.
- Negative projection.
- Procrastination.
- Poor self-image.
- Poor use of time.
- Go-It-Alone thinking.
- Prejudice.
- Jealousy.
- Unsupported bias.
- Lack of clear objectives.
- Resentment, anger, guilt.
- Lack of energy.
- Stubbornness (resist new ideas).
- Premature contentedness.
- Poor resource management.
- Thick-skinned (too insensitive).
- Thin-skinned (too sensitive).
- Inattention to detail.

❖ Excess attention to detail.

❖ Excesses.

❖ Lack of exercise.

❖ Poor listening habits.

❖ Poor setting of priorities.

❖ Inability to let go.

❖ "Me first" thinking.

My favorite barnacle was what one person I met called "rear-view mirror thinking." I asked her to explain. "Basically," she said, "it's trying to go forward by looking only at where I've been." Now, that's a barnacle worth scraping!

The process of discovering our own "barnacles" is one of personal renewal. It's a form of critical self-analysis, but with a less severe approach. It does, however, require each of us to accept a bit more responsibility for the things that keep us from reaching our potential. It requires an admission that few of us are able to do anything perfectly, and a commitment to look at how we could be better.

I've developed a formula I use for all of my speaking projects that I call RCR—review, critique, renew. After completing a speech or facilitating a workshop, I put it to the RCR test. I mentally replay the entire program and critique it in terms of presentation, content, audience reaction, and feedback. If you've ever spoken to a group, you know there are lots of ways to come up short of expectations! The Review stage of my formula helps me to identify those shortcomings. The Critique stage helps me to come to establish my role in creating those shortcomings. Did personal bias or prejudice keep me from considering other possibilities? Once I've identified my barnacles, I enter the Renewal stage, the process of scraping away behaviors and attitudes that may be slowing me down.

When I dumped all that literature in the trash can in Paris, I was acknowledging that much of what I had accumulated was nothing more than excess baggage I was unwilling to carry further. I had evaluated the cost, and determined that I was unwilling to pay it. The fact of the matter is that you cannot process into the future without paying a penalty for the excess baggage you intend to bring along. Good managers conduct frequent self-analysis to keep the process of renewal—and their careers—moving swiftly forward.

Turning failure into victory

1. Be positive! If you approach the process of identifying personal barnacles as a negative one, you'll run the risk of turning a productive experience into a traumatic one. Resist the temptation to beat yourself up, to see your shortcomings as failures. Learn and grow from past mistakes—those of others as well as your own.

2. Use a "Barnacle Log" to keep track of your commitments and your progress. Every time I do a self-evaluation, I note the date in the book along with areas that need improvement. The log helps me keep track of my commitments, while providing a record of my overall growth as a person.

3. Although I encourage people to make self-evaluations an ongoing process, it's important to take a more in-depth look several times a year. It could be that a major overhaul is needed. There's a nature center near where I live that provides a great setting for conducting the review. Several times a year, I like to pack a lunch and disappear for the day. The environment insures that the experience is both pleasant and productive.

4. Put together a game plan. Use your Barnacle Log to record the steps needed for improvement in a targeted area. Identify the resources you will need—people, books, tapes, and so on—and when you will begin. Set some timetables for review and hold yourself accountable for progress.

5. Use this process with your employees when you take them through the appraisal process. It will make the

process productive and positive, allowing them to view their shortcomings as opportunities for improvement.

Mess-Up No. 20

Failure to establish a viable business and personal network.

"One step by 100 persons is better than 100 steps by one person."

—Koichi Tsukamoto, founder and former . chairman of Wacoal Corp., Japan

A friend recently shared an interesting story with me. Faced with a staff problem he had never encountered before, he wasn't sure how he should proceed. He hired a consultant who quickly resolved the problem to the satisfaction of both staff and management. Several weeks later he was attending an educational workshop offered by his association. While chatting at lunch, one of the newer members asked if anyone could offer advice on a problem. The problem turned out to be so similar to the one my friend had just overcome that he was able to give the questioner some valuable advice. "I had to laugh," my friend told me, "I gave him $1,000 worth of information for free!" My friend didn't realize it at the time, but he had just been "networked."

The networking edge

Networking is the process of maximizing the experience of others, and any manager without a good network is in a "heap of hurt." A viable network of business and personal contacts enables you to extend your problem-solving capabilities by opening the door to people with similar frames of reference, experience, and problems. By tapping into the knowledge and experience of those who have dealt with the issues you face, you can avoid many of the pitfalls that have trapped others, and guide yourself toward successful options. In the example above, the new member with the problem discovered an important principle early in his career: If you can get good advice for free, grab it! In effect, that's what networking is all about.

Setting up a network of contacts is difficult for many because of a reluctance to "bother" people. Some people think of networking as the intellectual equivalent of siphoning gas out of a neighbor's car! In reality, networking is a "gas sharing" concept based on the assumption that we all run near empty on occasion when problems arise. We simply cannot allow our reluctance to keep us from taking advantage of this great resource. But remember, the key to successful networking is reciprocity.

Putting your network together

In putting together a workable network of peers, a number of steps can be followed to increase its effectiveness. Here are 10 points to consider for your next meeting or network opportunity.

1. **Network or suffer the consequences.** At the risk of sounding melodramatic, a failure to establish a successful network of colleagues and friends who can give you timely advice may keep you from reaching your goals.

2. **Be prepared.** Know in advance what information you want and who you hope to get it from. Set up appointments to meet key people, and plan to be where the action is!

3. **Be available.** Avail yourself of as many situations as possible in order to meet people.

4. **Practice your approach.** Most people find approaching a new contact or group intimidating. If the right blend of courtesy, attitude, respect, and enthusiasm is used, the approach should be right on target.

5. **Don't compromise the moment.** This should probably go unspoken, but when approaching a networking "opportunity" for the first time, smoking, drinking, profanity, and tasteless jokes are strongly discouraged.

6. **Pay attention.** I don't think there's anything as frustrating as giving information to someone who seems distracted or uninterested. Paying attention means giving the other person complete focus as payment for his or her time.

7. **Take good (but not copious) notes.** There's an old saying that the faintest notes are better than the best memory! I recommend carrying 3 x 5 cards in your pocket to every association or club meeting you attend. When you take notes, focus on key thoughts so you can jot the rest down later.

8. **Know how and when to weigh anchor.** As you build your network, you'll discover there are people ready and willing to give you volumes of information you may not need. Knowing when and how to disengage requires tact and diplomacy.

9. **Be a good value yourself.** A good piece of advice shared with me by a friend was profound in its simplicity. He told me, "If you're going to ask the advice of others, be worth the effort." The best networking relationships are reciprocal, with each member offering something in return.

10. **Stay in touch.** Like most relationships, the ones that grow are the ones in which we invest the most. To keep your network viable, make it a point to maintain correspondence with members of your network.

Turning failure into victory

1. Make up your own network list, starting with people whose ideas you value. You may want to add areas of expertise to the list as well if appropriate. Target individuals, whom you do not currently know, whose opinion you value. Then make meeting them a goal.

2. Make it a goal to add at least one new contact to your list monthly. Make it a qualified contact, not just someone you've met briefly. Establish a networking relationship by meeting that person for breakfast or lunch (your treat).

3. Remember that networking is not a parasitic activity. Look for ways to give as well as receive. I make it a point to send articles, notes, and so on, to a wide circle of contacts. It's rare that the recipients of these little values do not reciprocate.

4. Keep trying! You may encounter the occasional jerk who doesn't want to invest in others, but remember that his or her behavior is information about them, not you. Most people are glad to offer their advice.

5. Model the behavior you expect. Be a good network opportunity yourself.

Mess-Up No. 21

Failure to understand the impact of your personal style as a manager.

"Nothing succeeds like the appearance of success."

—Christopher Lasch,
The Culture of Narcissism

As I stumbled through the airport in Copenhagen, I was what the British call "knackered"—bone weary. I had just flown in from Norway on one of the most turbulent flights I'd ever experienced. Prior to the flight, I spent three hours killing time at the airport in Oslo while mechanics tried to fix a faulty valve. International travel after 9/11 can be tiring and stressful at best, but this particular trip went even beyond that. When I finally met with my host in Copenhagen that afternoon, all I wanted was a hot bath, a cup of tea, and an early bedtime. No such luck. As we gathered my belongings at the baggage carousel, my host informed me that he had reserved a table for us and two other guests at an exclusive restaurant in the city. "It's one of the finest in Europe," he informed me. Not wanting to offend him, I expressed polite enthusiasm.

Presentation counts!

That evening, refreshed by a quick shower and fortified with a stiff cup of Earl Grey, I joined my companions for what was to be the ultimate dining experience of my life. The restaurant was located in what had at one time been the catacombs under an old seminary. As we were being led to our table, I couldn't help but notice the walls, which featured a variety of stones jutting out at odd angles and lengths. Each of these protuberances had a lighted candle upon it, which gave the area a monastic feel. The waiters—each table had several—were dressed in tuxedos with a white linen draped over an arm. Each, I discovered, was a specialist able to guide the guest through the selection process.

As I recall, the food itself was superb. What I really remember, however, was the excellent presentation of each serving. From the first course to the plate of fruit and cheese at the end, everything was arranged with the skill of an artist. Later, I commented on the artistry of the chefs. "Presentation," my guest told me, "is half of the meal's flavor." Although I've had opportunity to eat in a number of outstanding restaurants over the years, this one stands out because of the care taken in how the food was presented to the customer. Fifteen years after this experience, I am still able to describe this memorable meal in detail.

The manager's style

Just like the presentation of a fine meal sets it apart, so does a manager's personal style set him or her apart from other managers. In this sense, a manager's style is the sum total of all the things that create impressions, things such as:

- ❖ Etiquette.
- ❖ Physical appearance.
- ❖ Penmanship.
- ❖ Clothes.
- ❖ Energy.
- ❖ Correspondence.
- ❖ Vocabulary.
- ❖ Relationship skills.

Like it or not, everything we do sends a message that defines us in someone else's eyes. If that someone else is the boss, these impressions could be either costly or beneficial, depending on the message received.

Little things matter

Over the years I have been amazed at the impact the smallest things can have on perceptions. I remember buying a new car and having the windshield cracked by a stone the day I drove it home. In Cincinnati, where I live, cracked windshields are a common occurrence. Because this was my fourth in two years, getting it fixed was no urgency. Several months later, as I was leaving work I happened to notice that my car was parked next to that of our company chairman. His was cleaned and polished and looked great. Mine, with a cracked windshield and mud-splattered hubcaps, looked like the second place finisher in a demolition derby. As I looked at the two vehicles, both less than a year old, I wondered what message each sent about its owner. I immediately had the windshield fixed, followed by a wash and wax job.

Communicating with your mouth shut

Studies indicate that as much as 55 percent of understanding comes from visual sources. Here are a few examples of nonverbal communication:

1. A handwritten note given to the boss is unreadable due to poor penmanship. The superior has to get clarification on a few parts.

2. A letter written to a customer and copied to the department head has typos and grammatical mistakes.

3. A manager shuffles through several piles of paperwork on his desk looking for the letter his boss needs right away.

4. A manager, when asked for his business card, extracts a limp, dog-eared version out of his wallet where it's resided for months. First thought, "Just how often does someone ask you for a card?"

5. A manager comes in on casual-dress day looking more casual than his coworkers.

6. For the umpteenth time, a manager can't drive at lunch because of the clutter in the back seat of his car.

7. An e-mail is virtually unreadable due to the manager's version of shorthand.

Each and every one of these scenarios conveys an undesirable message, no matter how competent a manager may be.

Turning failure into victory

1. Double-check the accuracy of all written communications, especially e-mail. I'm not sure who originated the idea that typos were acceptable in the interest of speed, but I would like to note that Outlook Express has spell check.

2. Consider everything you present—memos, reports, letters, and so on—to be the equivalent of a business card on your most important sales call. If handwritten, make extraordinary effort to make it readable and attractive. If your handwriting is a lost cause, make sure your written communication is typed.

3. Recognize the importance of good business etiquette. Don't be embarrassed to schedule a workshop on this topic if needed.

4. Remember, you are the product. The best automobile in the world will be hard to sell if it looks poor. Used car dealers understand this perfectly, and take great pains to present a clean and polished product. Good grooming sends a positive message about your product.

5. Ask yourself the question, "If I were someone else, how would I view me?" Better still, ask someone you trust to give you some honest (constructive) feedback on the message you're sending.

Mess-Up No. 22

Failure to take care of yourself.

"Going without sleep is as much a personal and public safety hazard as going to work drunk in the morning."

—Stanley Coren, *Sleep Thieves: An Eye-Opening Exploration Into the Science and Mysteries of Sleep*

The CEO of the company with which I was working came into the meeting late and took his customary seat at the head of the large conference table. The vice president of finance, halfway through his monthly update, paused briefly, than continued. When he finished, one by one the other department heads brought everyone up to date on what was happening in their area. As I looked around the room at the group assembled, I was surprised at the lack of energy displayed. Some people doodled, others fidgeted and others just stared out the window. As I looked at the faces around the table I suddenly realized, "Geez, these guys look wiped out."

As the meeting wore on, the telltale signs of fatigue became more pronounced. The purchasing manager, interrupted with a question about the status of some material, had difficulty remembering where she had left off. I glanced at the production manager sitting across the table from me and noticed him shudder in an attempt to rouse himself from a state of lethargy. His action brought a round of sniggering from the others. Afterwards, one manager told me, "That was a real snoozer." The problem wasn't the meeting. According to the National Sleep Foundation, if you're having trouble staying alert during boring or monotonous meetings, the problem is you.

Mom was right

On the surface, this Mess-Up would seem to be better grouped with such maternal intonations as looking both ways before crossing the street, eating your vegetables, and waiting an hour after lunch before going swimming. But before you shrug this off as a nonmanagement issue, consider this: CNN recently reported that sleep deprivation costs business $150 *billion* a year in higher stress and reduced workplace productivity.

After working with this particular company for several months, it was easy to see why the staff was worn out. Work weeks running 90 to 100 hours were common. Even if they got away at decent hours, PDAs, laptops, and cell phones served to stretch the workday well into night. And this group is not an exception. We're all working longer, while getting 20 percent less sleep than our grandparents did. Dr. James Maas, the author of *Power Sleep*, says that "when people are severely sleep deprived, they lose verbal and problem-solving skills, can't concentrate, and undergo rapid mood swings." Have you "barked" at anyone lately?

Catching up on the road

An interesting trend emerging involves the habits of managers on the road. According to a *Wall Street Journal* article, managers who travel are now opting for room service and an early bedtime instead of a night on the town. For years when I traveled, prime rib and late nights were common practice. Today, all I want is a salad and the opportunity to hit the sack at a decent hour. "Traveling is the only time I can get any rest," one manager told me. "Unless I think I might offend my host, I beg off going out as often as possible." Called "cocooning" by those in the travel industry, this desire to just stay in while on the road is recognition that a good rest is greatly valued by today's business manager.

There is a cost

Managers who become sleep deprived expose themselves to a wide variety of problems ranging from reduced efficiency and effectiveness (studies indicate lack of sleep can lower creative capacity by as much as 30 percent), to chronic fatigue. When a person fails to get the proper amount of rest, the body tends to "cycle down" until exhaustion sets in. Sleep obtained at this point, while beneficial, does not take us back to a fully restored level. When the cycle is repeated, we sink a little further because we don't start with a "full tank" to begin with. As the cycle repeats itself, our sleep resources are depleted to the point that chronic fatigue kicks in. I know, it happened to me.

Like many businesspeople, I took great pride in my ability to work as long and hard as I chose. I derived a perverse pleasure in being the first one to arrive at work and the last one to leave. My work habits were intense as well. I wanted maximum output from each minute, and pushed myself relentlessly to achieve it. On the weekends, I transferred my intensity to projects around the house. When the time came to "pay the piper" for my transgressions, the price was severe. I battled chronic fatigue for nearly five years before regaining full strength.

The sleep deficit problem

The bottom line is this: Regardless of what you may feel about your capacity for work, you cannot bring your best to the office every day if you are failing to get a proper amount of rest. What's the proper amount? Studies used to suggest that it varied with each individual, but recent research is reinforcing the old wisdom that eight hours of sleep a night is probably right for everyone. By getting a sufficient amount of rest, a higher level of performance can be achieved that will more than offset the time committed to a full night's sleep. It's how you, as a competent manager and leader, keep your ax sharp.

Turning failure into victory

1. Recognize that sleep, like operating capital, is a resource that must be maintained. Just as a company guards against the poor use of its financial resources, so you must guard against the careless expending of physical ones. Avoid getting into "sleep debt."

2. Develop a procedure. Studies indicate that by establishing a regular routine for going to bed and rising, the human body can maximize its opportunity to restore itself. Visit *www.sleepfoundation.org* for more information on developing a good (consistent) sleep routine.

3. Refrain from watching CNN or Fox News before going to sleep, as these activities stimulate brain activity, making it difficult for your body to relax. Allow a wind-down time after these activities before going to bed.

4. Establish a recovery day. Although most experts say it's best to establish a regular routine, a "catch-up day" can help. Pick a day of your workweek to be your get-away-early, get-to-bed-early day. You'll be surprised at the benefit.

5. Take a nap! When Ronald Reagan was president, a lot of attention was given to his penchant for afternoon naps. The president, however, was doing nothing more than what good managers always do—maximizing resources. Naps can be an excellent way to do so.

Mess-Up No. 23

Failure to relentlessly prepare for the future.

"In times of change, learners inherit the earth, while the learned find themselves beautifully equipped to deal with a world that no longer exists."

—Eric Hoffer, author of
The Ordeal of Change

My oldest daughter had just walked across the stage to pick up her bachelor's degree, and was heading down the aisle to return to her seat. As I prepared to take a close-up photo, she gave me a euphoric smile and shouted, "I'm never opening another book again!" It's with great relief that I report she was only kidding. In fact, she was the driving force in creating the first annual Kentucky Book Festival. She's an avid reader, and constantly looks for ideas and concepts that will help her in her work. Unfortunately, she's a statistical minority.

Studies indicate that reading is a lost art for the majority of college graduates, with more than 70 percent never reading another book in their area of expertise. There may have been a time in the past when this behavior may not have affected the success of a businessperson. But in today's fast-changing workplace, this is a formula for failure.

Sustainable advantage

Arie deGeus, the former head of planning for Royal Dutch Shell once said: "The ability to learn faster than your competitors may be the only sustainable competitive advantage." The reason is simple: A manager's potential for success is rooted in his or her capacity to solve problems. That skill is heavily dependent on the manager's commitment to relentlessly prepare for the future. Let me illustrate by adapting a concept from Professor John Kotter at Harvard.

Let's assume three people join a company on the same day. Because their skills and background are largely the same, we'll give each 100 PSC (Problem Solving Capacity) units. The first person, I'll call him David, is a hard worker who puts in a lot of hours. Like the vast majority of workers, David puts little effort into continued learning. He is counting on his effort (hours worked) to grow his career.

Our second worker, Elizabeth, works hard as well, but also manages to maintain a reading program that keeps her abreast of what's happening in business as well as her industry. She tries, when time permits, to attend seminars and workshops. Each year she sets a goal of reading 25 books, although she has been falling short of that mark. As a result of her learning commitment, Elizabeth manages to maintain an annual growth rate of 4 percent, well ahead of most coworkers.

Our third worker, we'll call him Rolf, is an aggressive learner. He has a voracious reading appetite, actively seeks learning opportunities, asks a lot of questions, and stays curious about the world around him. He examines his failures for what each might reveal, and he reflects on his triumphs for the same reason. He has a written personal learning plan to hold himself accountable. As a result, he is able to maintain an annual growth rate of 9 percent.

Let's fast forward 25 years. David, who began with 100 PSC units, now has less than that amount due to knowledge obsolescence. Elizabeth, learning at a rate of 4 percent, has increased her 100 units to 256, making her two and a half times more capable than David as a problem solver. Rolf, on the other hand, growing at 9 percent, has increased his PSC units to over 862, or nearly three and a half times Elizabeth.

In a world where information is available to everyone and knowledge obsoletes itself at an alarming rate, Rolf has lifted himself above the competition simply by making learning a lifelong passion. By relentlessly preparing for the future, Rolf made sure he was prepared to assume the role of a capable solver of problems.

Extending product life

In his book, *Good-To-Great*, Jim Collins interviewed Darwin Smith, the CEO responsible for turning Kimberly Clark from a stodgy old paper company into a world-class performer. Collins asked the now-retired executive what the secret was of his leadership prowess. Smith thought a moment then replied, "I never stopped trying to become qualified for the job."

Managers who will have the answers to the questions presented by the competitive pressures of the 21st century are those who are committed to a program of continuous learning. These people understand that the continuous acquisition of new ideas and information is as critical to their future as staying current on the latest medical procedures is to a physician. Unless they stay sufficiently ahead, the end may well be at hand.

A lesson from Honest Abe

One of my favorite stories is about a man who challenged Abe Lincoln to a log splitting contest. As the contest progressed, the man noticed that Lincoln had stopped to take a rest. Determined to build a lead, he continued without rest until lunch. When he paused at lunch, he was shocked to see that Lincoln's stack was larger than his own. Wondering how that could possibly be, he decided to chop through the lunch hour. He continued his frenetic pace until the end of the day, when the two men stopped to compare output. Lincoln had beaten him by a substantial margin. Tired and frustrated, the man asked Lincoln how he had done it. "Every time I looked in your direction," the man said, "you were taking a break." Lincoln smiled and replied, "Every time I took a break, I sharpened my ax."

Turning failure into victory

1. Make learning a lifelong commitment. At age of 80, Michelangelo's motto in life was "Ancora Imparo," Latin for "And still I learn." Despite god-like status, Michelangelo considered it essential that he keep studying, learning, and growing.

2. The Internet is awesome, but take time to rediscover the library. Most libraries lend as many DVDs and CDs as books and periodicals, so I always stock up before a trip. Ask the librarian what's available and when the next seminar on library use will be held. Then, attend it.

3. Develop a personal learning plan complete with mission statement ("With a commitment to lifelong learning, I will continually increase my capacity to create, innovate, and solve problems"). Include goals and dated action items.

4. Find a learning accountability partner. Share with them your learning objectives and goals, and ask them to hold you responsible for meeting them. This works best when you can fill the same role for each other.

5. Learn from a wide range of material. Include your area of expertise, but do not limit yourself to that area. The broader your knowledge base, the better.

Part 6:
Problem Solving

Mess-Up No. 24

Failure to make innovation a deliverable.

"We are powerfully imprisoned in these Dark Ages simply by the terms in which we have been conditioned to think."

—R. Buckminster Fuller,
inventor and designer

Suppose you applied for a new job, and one of the requirements was the ability to generate 200 new ideas per year. Would you be able to accept the position?

This question is one I often ask participants in my workshops. Surprisingly, no more than a handful answer yes to this question. In order to improve the response, I add that the ideas don't even have to be good! This doesn't change the responses. I then remind the group that this is only 3/4 of an idea per workday, but this doesn't seem to impress anyone. When I then ask the group, by a show of hands, how many of them feel that they have some degree of creativity, the number of raised hands actually declines! Then I ask how many feel they are above average in intelligence. Every hand in the room is raised.

Creativity is underrated

It strikes me odd that at a period in time when companies need ideas more than ever to respond to the changes cascading upon them, most of these companies are neither teaching nor requiring creative output. More attention is being paid to whether employees are arriving on time than to whether or not they have suggestions for improving productivity. In a performance appraisal I was giving an employee, under the category "Suggestions for Growth," I noted that she could be of greater value to the company if she would increase her ability to offer innovative options for improving her area. The next day she came into my office, visibly upset.. "What's the matter?" I asked. On the verge of tears she replied, "I'm going to have to quit my job. I'm just not a creative person," she sniffled.

A new emphasis is needed

For too long, employers have allowed their employees to duck the creativity issue. The truth of the matter is that everybody is creative. Some people have a greater capacity for creativity because they've trained themselves to be so. One young engineer I know develops a top-10 list daily on subjects ranging from why chickens cross the road, to ways to skin a cat. His coworkers can't wait to see what he comes up with. This creative exercise, designed to get a few chuckles, has a wonderful byproduct. It trains him to look for new ideas on a daily basis. Not surprisingly, he's regarded as one of the most creative people in his company, a role he takes pride in. Companies that require creative output from employees will be the ones with the greatest ability to reinvent themselves when market pressures dictate it. And they *will* dictate it. As Jeff Immelt, the chairman of GE says, "Its time to release the mad scientists!"

More than adequate power!

I was conducting a workshop recently on managing change and asked the attendees this question: "Is there enough idea-generating power in this room to produce results?" Eyes looked in every direction but mine, much the way my university students avoided eye contact, thinking it would surely lead to a question from me. I asked them to break into groups of five and to work together on an exercise I had taken from creative thinking expert Roger von Oech, author of *A Kick in the Seat of the Pants*. The assignment: Design the perfect coffee cup for use at the beach. At first, everyone thought the assignment to be my idea of a joke. When they discovered it wasn't, they got busy considering the options.

After giving them half an hour to work on the problem, I asked each group to select an "engineer" to describe the features of their cup. I also asked them to select a marketing manager to convert those features into benefits. What followed was a lot of laughter (a key ingredient in the creative process), a lot of energy, and some of the fanciest coffee cups you could imagine. Since cost was not a factor, cups sported such built-in accessories as a BlackBerry, MP3, and GPS tracking so you would know where you were on the beach! Other innovations included a sunscreen dispenser and HDTV. Few, it seemed, were ideally suited for drinking coffee! By the end of the exercise, however, most people had a different view of themselves as idea generators.

Define the creative process

Most people's perception of the creative process is that it involves snatching some new and innovative idea out of thin air. They see it as a sort of lightning bolt striking randomly. The definition of creativity I like the best is one offered by Mike Vance, the former Dean of Disney

University. Vance defines creativity as the making of the new and the rearranging of the old in a new way. While the first part of his definition is important, it's the latter that holds the most hope for future growth.

Creative alibis

When asked to contribute new ideas, many people are at their creative best in thinking up reasons why they should be excused from the assignment. Here's a partial list of some of the more common excuses people offer for their lack of creative output.

"I'm just not creative." Whenever someone makes this statement my response is, "Horsefeathers!" Okay, maybe not. But if you're a living, breathing human being, you are creative. There's no way around it. The potential is denied to no one. Science tells us that if you can laugh at a joke, you're creative. The same part of our brain that interprets a joke and causes us to laugh generates creative output. So if you can laugh, you can't use this alibi!

"I'm afraid my idea won't work." Thank goodness Thomas Edison didn't feel this way. Edison seldom invented anything on the first try. His incandescent light bulb failed to work thousands of times before success was achieved. It took Edison 10 years and more than 50,000 experiments to perfect his alkaline storage battery. Typically, Edison didn't see these as failures. "I succeeded in discovering 50,000 ways not to invent an alkaline battery," he'd say. A key ingredient in successful idea generation is the ability to defer judgment. Idea generation and evaluation should never occur at the same time. Let your ideas flow freely, and then take the time to determine their viability and value. And if you're worried about coming up with a dumb idea, take comfort in the thought that people who are a lot smarter than you have done that as well.

"I just don't have the time." This is probably the most often cited excuse people give when they don't want to do *anything!* The truth is, we'll always find time for the things we appreciate and want to do. Once creativity reaches that level of value in our minds, the time will be available.

"It's really not something I'm supposed to be doing." The first time someone made this comment to me, I almost choked. I asked the woman what she meant. "Well," she replied, "I don't think my company wants anything from me but the usual things." I'm not sure what the "usual things" are, but I bet a creative individual could make them more productive, resulting in greater success for the organization as well as for the individual.

Reasons abound for why people do not contribute more to their companies in terms of creative output. But the need for that output has never been greater. The need for creativity goes well beyond the customer's demand for the latest and greatest. Today's companies need creativity to manage change, to respond to an erratic and uncertain market, and to respond to the demands for greater productivity in every department. Without a fresh flow of ideas to meet these needs, businesses will lose their competitive edge.

Turning failure into victory

1. Prime the pump by acknowledging creative effort, not outcome. Create a positive environment where problem-solving and idea generation are openly valued. Once people begin to realize that creativity is valued and is expected to be a routine part of their job, they will become more comfortable with the concept.

2. Teach people there are no bad ideas. Emphasize the invention-extension concept whereby people build off each other's ideas. While initially an idea generated may have little merit, mentioning it may spark an idea that does. Most breakthroughs are an iterative process.

3. Encourage your staff to practice being creative. Periodically give your group hypothetical problems to solve. Instead of looking for practical answers, challenge them to "step outside the box" (rational thought) and come up with offbeat—even outrageous—options.

4. Establish creative requirements for your department. Let your staff know that part of their annual performance evaluations will be based on their ability to generate ideas for doing things better in their department, or even throughout the organization. Encourage everyone to maintain a creativity log.

5. Allow people to have some fun, but remind them of the practical side of innovation. Thomas Edison said he didn't want to invent anything that wouldn't sell. As Drucker notes, "A novelty only creates amusement."

Mess-Up No. 25

Failure to exhibit the "Wright Stuff" when it comes to solving problems.

"We could not help thinking that many of their troubles might have been avoided and that others might have been overcome by the adoption of more adequate methods."

—Wilbur Wright, inventor

A 20-year fascination with the Wright brothers culminated in my second book, *The Wright Way: 7 Problem-Solving Principles From The Wright Brothers That Can Make Your Business Soar* (AMACOM). The book takes a close look at the techniques the brothers used to solve what most people, including the *New York Times*, thought was an unsolvable problem: heavier-than-air manned flight. In fact, it was believed to be so unsolvable, many interested in the problem kept it to themselves for fear of losing their jobs should such lunacy be discovered by employers!

First in flight

I often wondered why success had fallen to the Wrights when so many others had failed. How were two young bicycle builders from Dayton, Ohio, able to do what the best financed engineers and brightest scientists of the day could not? The answer, I discovered, lay in a remarkable blend of personality traits, family beliefs, and a problem-solving model I call *The Wright Way*. Here's a brief look at some of the principles:

Principle: A passionate belief in purpose. Have you ever believed in something so strongly that you were willing to pay any price to achieve it? Studies indicate that few of us have that kind of life-defining fervor. But when it comes to solving problems, that kind of passion is essential to keeping things moving forward when obstacles appear. The fervor of the Wrights was revealed in a letter Wilbur wrote to noted aviationist Octave Chanute in May of 1900. "I'm afflicted with the belief that man can fly," Wright wrote. "My disease (desire to fly) has increased in severity and I feel that it will soon cost me an increased amount of money, if not my life." That belief, that incredible power of purpose, was a force multiplier that carried the Wright brothers through times of trial. And there were plenty of those.

Principle: Divergent thought/common purpose. Tom Crouch wrote in *The Bishop's Boys*, his excellent profile of the Wright brothers, that Wilbur and Orville were very effective at arguing through to the solution of a problem. It's a shame many businesses today fail to promote a good scrap among well-meaning men and women of imagination. Disagreement is not always conflict. The Wrights learned how to disagree and took great delight in arguing with each other, but with a purpose. "I love to scrap with Orv," Wilbur once remarked. "It brings out new ways of looking at things and helps to round off the corners." Out of their "scraps" came the seeds of success, the many ideas that would fuel their drive to conquer the sky. By playing off each other's ideas, new options were revealed.

Principle: Problem solving is a process. The problems facing the Wrights were innumerable. Not only were they inventing the world's first heavier-than-air flying machine, but the science of flying as well. Lift, pitch, roll. All would need to be discovered before they could be mastered. It was often necessary for the Wrights to invent the equipment needed just to invent another component. They were equal to the task. Tom Crouch writes of Wilbur: "He was the perfect engineer—isolating a basic problem, defining it in the most precise terms, and identifying the missing bits of information that would enable him to solve it."

While others buried themselves in excessive detail, the Wrights cleared away the clutter. Hours were spent defining the problem in its simplest terms, followed by brainstorming sessions to develop options. Alternatives were examined in their entirety until all reason had been driven from them. Those that remained were tested, over and over, until they were adopted, adapted, or abandoned in favor of more promising options.

Principle: Rigid flexibility. Because they relied so heavily on the calculations of others, early aviators would fail time and again to put their machines into the sky. The Wrights, however, were wedded to no school of thought, calculations, or precedents. When their lift calculations failed to provide the expected results, the Wrights threw out all prior data and started over. They invented a wind tunnel and ran their own tests. Rather than lock themselves into rigid thought, the Wrights cultivated the ability to look at things from many directions. They were always willing to back off a bad option, no matter how much time had been spent pursuing it. While rigid in their pursuit of the goal, they were flexible in the means to achieve it.

Principle: Dogged persistence. Time and again, the Wrights would haul their gliders to the top of Kill Devil Hill on the Outer Banks of North Carolina. Orville and Wilbur would take turns as pilot, sailing powerless over the edge of the huge sand dune. Many of the flights ended with a mouthful of sand, or with an even closer call. Afterwards, the 112 pound glider would be carried back up the hill where the process was repeated. How many times? Thousands, each one carefully logged and studied.

Principle: Teamwork ("we" and "us"). When asked about his sons, Bishop Wright commented, "They are equal in their inventions, neither claiming any superiority over the other." What they did, they did as a team—Wilbur the engineer and scientist, Orville the machinist and craftsman. They designed and built the world's first airplane together. And when it came time to fly it, a coin toss would decide who would go first. When Orville lifted off that cold December day in 1903, Wilbur ran alongside, steadying the wing and giving encouragement. It took both to make it happen.

Principle: A willingness to take (reasoned) risk. Orville and Wilbur Wright were cautious men, unwilling to proceed on the basis of shaky or incomplete information. Especially Wilbur. He would often chastise his brother for not taking all of the necessary precautions. Despite their care, danger was a constant companion. In the fall of 1908, Orville suffered serious injuries in a crash while demonstrating the Wright Flyer to the army. Lt. Thomas Selfridge, a passenger, became the world's first airplane fatality that day. Wright would never recover from his injuries, yet he continued flying—in pain—for years. The Wrights, fully aware of the potential consequences, were willing to pay the price to achieve their goal. They weren't risk takers as much as opportunity takers.

Principle: Forever learning. Although neither of the Wrights had graduated from high school, both learned at an early age to read critically. They continued throughout their work to be avid students, not just of the science of flight, but of many disciplines. Particular attention was paid to the failure of others. They carefully examined the works of people in many divergent fields. Their breakthrough ideas came from a variety of sources. Even simple childhood toys inspired them. The Wrights believed that ideas were all around them and never missed out on a chance to learn.

Turning failure into victory

1. Break a problem down into manageable segments. As the Wrights learned early on, they could not solve the problem of flight in a single step.

2. Define the problem you are addressing. This was always the critical first step with the Wrights. Other aviationists of the time were successful in solving the wrong problem.

3. Define the limiting factors that may inhibit your ability to solve your problem. The Wrights, financed by profits generated from their bicycle business, understood limited resources, and built that into their plan.

4. Develop a list of possible alternatives. Don't be satisfied with the first right answer! The Wrights, knowing so much was at stake, tried to establish a wide range of options for each problem addressed.

5. Choose carefully. For the Wright brothers, the choices they made were often matters of life or death. Options were carefully weighed before making their decision.

Mess-Up No. 26

Failure to teach employees to contend for their ideas.

"Where there is much desire to learn, there of necessity will be much arguing..."

—John Milton, English Poet

Carol was a bit apprehensive as she walked into her company's board room for her first manager's meeting. As the new marketing manager, she was excited about her opportunity, and had put considerable effort into her report to fellow executives. She understood the importance of first impressions, and had carefully planned every detail of her presentation. As she took her place at the table, one of the sales managers, observing the desktop published handouts in a neat stack in front of her, commented, "I hope you're not one of those over-achievers." "Well," Carol replied, "I'm excited about sharing my ideas, and I want to present them well." "Good luck," the man said, "you're going to need it."

While they were waiting for the president to arrive, the sales manager leaned over to Carol and, surreptitiously covering his mouth said, "Let me give you a little advice about our president." Carol turned to listen. "Keep an eye on Chuck's forehead during the meeting," he said. Confused, Carol asked why. "Well," the sales manager continued, "he has this one vein on his forehead that really swells up when he's getting ready to explode." "If it starts getting bigger while you're talking, it's probably a good idea to change the subject." Thanking him for the tip, Carol began to wonder what she had gotten herself into.

Fifteen minutes later, the president came into the room, slammed a pile of papers on the table and said, "Let's get this over with." Pointing to the VP of finance he barked, "Let's start with the numbers." Then he added, "The rest is irrelevant anyway." As the meeting unfolded, it became obvious to Carol that her fellow managers were not interested in prolonging the ordeal. Reports were brief, and offered little in the way of new ideas. As manager after manager gave a terse, uninspiring report, Carol quietly pulled the reports in front of her off the table and slipped them into her briefcase. "Good move," the manager beside her whispered.

Stark contrast

When this story was shared with me by Carol (not her real name), I couldn't help but recall another manager's meeting I attended several months earlier. To familiarize me with their culture, my client had asked me to observe his engineering team "in action." The meeting, to say the least, was eye-opening. Instead of a formal agenda, the session began with a problem scribbled on a white board. What followed was a spirited debate over the best way to resolve the issue. Participants showed little hesitation in challenging each other's ideas, and at times it got pretty intense. By the end of the meeting, however, the group had identified not one but several options for its customer. As the meeting broke up, I was amazed to see former "combatants" walking out talking amicably about an upcoming company picnic.

The difference between the two companies was the difference in their cultures. One company had created an environment where people felt free to contend for their ideas. More than that, they were *expected* to contend for their ideas. They had succeeded in creating an environment where people felt safe "airing out" their thoughts. They knew that their ideas might come under fire, but that their self-esteem wouldn't. The culture at Carol's company was just the opposite. She and her comanagers felt anything but safe, and the results showed it.

Going along to get along

In business today, it seems we've lost the ability to contest each other's ideas. In the name of political correctness, we've made the pursuit of pleasantness more important than the generation of new ideas. We tolerate every kind of diversity except diversity of thought. Going along to get along is more important than providing customers with an assortment of viable options. Sometimes people are reluctant to engage in the process because of trust issues. They question the true motives of leaders. Others equate conflict with winning and losing, and fear that "losing" will lead to unwanted changes.

In assessing your department or company to see if spirited debate (constructive conflict) might be a useful tool, here are a few questions to consider about current culture:

❖ Is the agenda open and public, or private and hidden?

❖ Is the goal improvement, or winning the "fight?"

❖ Do participants feel safe, or exposed?

❖ Is participation high, or tentative and constrained?

❖ Are people listening, or forming responses?

❖ Is information shared, or hoarded as "ammo?"

Once you've answered these questions, you should have a good idea whether the conflict in your company will be constructive or destructive. If it's constructive, forge ahead! If not, there are probably more pressing matters for you to address first.

The benefits of teaching employees to contend for their ideas are considerable. It's not only an effective way to surface new ideas and options, but to explore their ramifications as well. Subjecting ideas to spirited debate also helps to reshape them through the process of invention-extension. Further, contending for ideas forces people to do their homework, to really ponder their concepts and be more original in their thinking.

The best companies, rather than avoiding conflict, embrace it. They see it as a vital energy source that feeds everything from new product ideas to the marketing strategies that sell them.

Turning failure into victory

1. To implement contenting (constructive conflict) in your company or department, first think about the emotional climate and maturity of your staff. If there is any friction or unresolved conflict, address that first.

2. Communicate clearly what constructive conflict is all about, assuring team members that while their ideas may come under attack, they won't.

3. Prime the pump by giving your team less volatile topics to consider. As trust and confidence grow, begin to introduce more challenging subjects.

4. Encourage participants to really listen to the other parties, regardless of their feelings toward their position or idea. Remember, the goal isn't to win the argument, but to surface truth.

5. Allow some time for participants to come back together after the discussion. One of the keys to making this work is the ability of people to contend for their ideas, but conclude the session as a team.

Mess-Up No. 27

Failure to have a professional problem solving strategy.

"No problem can stand the assault of sustained thinking."

—Voltaire

In my seminars, I often ask if there are golfers in the class. Of course there always are, so my next question is, "Do you have a strategy for hitting the ball straight?" Once in a while I get a group that's *really* into the sport, and I spend the next half hour trying to regain control of the program! For the most part, however, advice is limited to the following: Use an over-lapping grip, flex your knees, keep your arm straight, keep your head down, and follow through. Satisfied that we've covered the basics, I ask my group one more question: "How many of you have a formal strategy for making a decision?"

I find it fascinating that people give so much attention to their golf swing, but are satisfied to just "hack away" when it comes to making an important business decision—especially because making decisions is such an important component of management. Former mayor of New York City, Rudy Giuliani, who knows a thing or two about problem-solving, says people follow solutions. If that's the case (and it is), we can assume that companies that solve problems will grow, and those that solve them best will grow the most. Given the importance of this discipline, isn't a reasoned approach warranted?

A professional approach

Most of the decisions a manager makes in an average day are Automatic Decisions, those that require little thought. The brain has a considerable bank of data stored on these, and really doesn't need our participation. For example, expense reports need to be completed and turned in each week. This type of decision requires little deliberation. Plug the data into the right slots and you're done. Although automatic decisions comprise the greatest number of decisions a manager makes, they're not the ones we're paid to make.

The two types of problems managers deal with most are *linear* (directed) and *non-linear* (non-directed) problems. Non-linear problems are those for which no set procedure exists to guide the problem-solver. These problems are dependant on a manager's ability to use innovation, intuition, and imagination as tools in developing possible solutions. A manager's risk-taking propensity and flexibility are key elements.

Linear problems are those for which a procedure exists to guide the solver. The majority of problems managers face fall in this group. If there's a problem with employee performance, for example, a set of guidelines exists—verbal warning, written warning, suspension, and so on—to guide the manager's actions. Although they can also be of use in addressing non-linear issues, the best tool a manager has for solving linear problems is a problem-solving model.

Problem solving models are processes for making decisions that lead to good solutions. There are a number of models available to managers including Force Field Analysis, SWOT Analysis, Cost/Benefit Analysis, and Decision Matrix, to name a few. Six Sigma and Lean Manufacturing practices are, in part, problem-solving models as well. The model used most often, however, is the classic Seven Step Method. Here's a brief look at this useful decision-making tool:

Step 1: Identify and select the real problem. This is easily the most important step in the process, because how the problem is framed impacts everything that follows. The greatest tendency here is to identify a symptom as the problem, or to define the problem in terms of a preferred outcome. Determining the solution criteria here is useful. Suppose a company is producing 800 widgets a day and needs to increase it to 1,000. The *solution criteria* is the *desired state* minus the *current one*. The real problem is not how to produce 1,000 widgets a day, but how to produce 200 more.

Step 2: Gather information on the problem. This step is the "grunt work" part of the process. In order to make an informed decision, you first have to be informed. Gather everything you practically can relative to the problem: Reports, data, ideas, suppositions, and so on. The key here is to watch out for personal bias. In other words, don't fixate on data which support a preconceived idea where you feel the answer should be. It's important to remember that there's a law of diminishing returns on information. Make sure the cost of the information (time, money, opportunity) does not exceed the benefit.

Step 3: Analyze the problem to identify root causes. The most common error in problem solving is defining problems in terms of their solutions. People think they are expressing problems when they are actually stating a potential solution.

Step 4: Generate possible solutions. The fourth step in the process is to explore alternative solutions to the problem identified in step one. As potential options are surfaced, ask yourself, "Will this solution make enough of a difference to matter?" Evaluate each in terms of its cost effectiveness, potential pitfalls, and whether it fits current circumstances.

Step 5: Select the best option (solution). After evaluating each alternative generated in step four, ask yourself if one solution stands out from all the others as having the greatest number of advantages or the least number of disadvantages. If one comes to the forefront, make sure that it satisfies the following criteria: Does it make political sense? Does it put anyone at risk or jeopardize their safety? Is it financially feasible? Will it compromise the environment? It is ethically sound? If it fails any of these criteria, eliminate it from consideration.

Step 6: Implement the solution. After selecting the best alternative, the option selected should be put in use. Having determined the objective and the best way to achieve it, identify what resources will be needed. Begin by developing an action plan which answers the "who, what, where, when, and why" questions. Once the plan is complete, use it to implement the solution.

Step 7: Evaluate (verify) the results. The final step in this model involves determining if the solution selected is the most appropriate one. First, monitor the solution to see if it fits the problem specified. Is it still the best solution? Are there any undesirable side effects? If it fails to solve the problem, has the situation changed? Will additional resources help? If all the answers are satisfactory, move on to your next challenge!

Despite its importance, studies indicate that the use of a model to solve problems or make a key decision is one of the least practiced of all management tools. Perhaps it's the time it takes, or maybe the lack of discipline to execute the steps. In a world that places a premium on getting it right, the effort required to use this tool more than compensates the user. Let's face it, you can only guess right so many times. Might as well be a professional.

Turning failure into victory

1. First, think about it. Before seeking other points of view, take time to ponder the problem yourself. Pondering is the art of thinking clearly about a problem, suspending judgment as you consider all possibilities. Resist jumping to conclusions, but develop an original, untainted perspective first.

2. Lay a firm foundation. Correctly identifying the problem is the crucial first-step, so give this portion of the model the time and attention it deserves. If it's crooked at the bottom, it will be crooked at the top! As Charles Kettering says, "A problem well stated is a problem half solved."

3. Options! Options! Options! It's been said that there's nothing quite as dangerous as a man with an idea, if it's the only one he's got! To give yourself the best chance for success, develop a good pool of alternative solutions. Avoid being satisfied with the first "right answer."

4. Identify barriers. In looking at any problem-solving scenario, ask yourself what obstacles might have to be overcome or compensated for. These obstacles can be

external (market driven), internal (company driven), or personal (bias). Most of these will center on limited resources: Time, money, and access (to people).

5. Be a professional. Decision making and problem-solving are key elements of a manager's responsibilities. Make good decisions, and your company prospers. Make poor ones, and your career falters. Are you willing to leave either to a toss of the coin?

Mess-Up No. 28

Failure to take reasoned risks when needed.

"Some companies are better than others at tapping the creative potential of their people, while others stamp it out at its first emergence."

—Rosabeth Moss Kanter,
author of *Change Masters*

I was interviewing a purchasing manager for a major manufacturer recently, and asked her what she thought was the most important criteria in selecting a supplier. She smiled and said, "Whether or not I will lose my job." Noting the puzzled look on my face she added, "It's really simple. If I place an order with a company and that order goes past due, or gets lost or has quality problems—it's my job that's on the line. If our production manager finds his line down because of one of my suppliers, I guarantee you he's coming after me and not the supplier." "It sounds to me," I commented, "like the most important criteria is the old CYA factor." "You got it," she said.

Concerned with her reply, I continued. "Doesn't a philosophy of covering your rear end keep you from considering new sources of supply that might be able to reduce your costs?" I asked. "Yes, that happens all the time," she replied. "I get unsolicited proposals all the time from sources that run 10 to 20 percent lower than what I'm paying now, but I just pass them up." "Doesn't that hamper your ability to compete?" I asked again. "Yes, I suppose in the big picture sense it does," she said, looking ready for a new topic to discuss. "But the simple fact," she continued, "is that this company provides no incentives for taking a risk. And believe me, there are ample opportunities to get shot down if you mess up. I want to buy from suppliers that expose me to the least amount of risk and criticism."

Risky business

What will it take to succeed in business in a new age of uncertainty and challenge? I directed this question to a group of 100 senior managers, asking each to break it down into six key attributes. Although the ideas shared were packaged in a variety of ways, almost everyone agreed on the six main attributes. The businesses that would succeed, they said, would be characterized by speed-to-market, a turn-on-a-dime mentality, learning ability, passion for service, ability to reinvent themselves as needed, and a commitment to energizing employees.

When I thought about these attributes later, I realized that there was one common thread among them: a company's propensity for taking risks. Without a management team in place that feels comfortable with the need to take reasoned risks, a company cannot possibly develop the speed, responsiveness, and flexibility needed to compete effectively in an economy that values the latest and greatest of anything. Unless an organization has committed itself to following the best judgment of well-informed managers, it cannot be a real player in this economy.

A company's propensity for taking risks is determined by both the culture of the organization and the risk-taking style of its managers. All things being equal, culture usually wins. If a culture is regimented and frowns on personal innovation and risk-taking, the chances of risk-taking subcultures forming within the organization are not great. Companies with cultures that force employees to adopt an assembly-line mentality to their work often compromise the very edge they need to compete.

The cost of risks averted

Several years ago I was being guided on a tour of a customer's plant by its production manager. I told him I was impressed with the cleanliness of his operation. "Thank you," he said. "We're very proud of our facility." As we headed to the break area for coffee, the man turned to me and said, "I don't know if they told you, but we ship more than 99 percent of our orders on time." I told him that was an extraordinary achievement, and that his team should be congratulated. "It's something we're proud of," he said, "something we all strive to make happen every day. Taking care of customers is what it's all about."

Later that same day, I had an opportunity to meet with the company's vice president of sales. "I was pretty impressed with your production manager," I said. "Not many companies can boast of such a fantastic on-time shipment record." I was surprised when he responded that he thought the on-time shipment record was too high. "I'm not sure I understand how an increase in missed deliveries helps your sales," I commented. "In our business," he responded, "many orders are placed with whomever has the shortest lead times. If you play it safe all the time, a lot of business will go somewhere else." I asked him to elaborate on this.

Another perspective

"Suppose you were a high jumper," he began. "On your first approach to the bar, you easily clear the height. What do you do?" "You raise the bar and jump again," I replied. "That all depends," he answered, "on what your objective is. If your objective is to minimize risk, you leave the bar at where it is and continue jumping at that height. If you really want to be sure, you could even lower it." "That doesn't seem like much of a challenge," I said. "Well," he replied, "that's another objective altogether. If you're trying to see how high you can go, you would choose to raise the bar." "Isn't it imperative in your business—in any business—that you continue to get better?" I asked. "Yes it is," he said, "but there's risk associated with improvement, and some people don't like risk."

"Shipping 99 percent of our orders on time is the equivalent of never raising the bar," the sales manager continued. "Because our production manager is a risk averter, we miss out on a lot of business because we're not aggressive enough on our lead times. You have to look at it in terms of the overall objective," he said. "If we were more aggressive on the dates we promise, we might increase our sales by 20 percent. Our on-time delivery percentage might go down, but the increase in sales would more than offset that liability." I was getting his point, but responded that I was still uncomfortable with the idea of shipping late.

"All of business is about trade-offs," the man said. "That's why there are risks involved. The goal of business isn't just growth, it's *maximum* growth. I'm not asking the production manager to be reckless with his delivery promises, just to take reasoned risk."

The case for reasoned risk-taking

Whenever I make the case for increasing risk-taking, I always add the word "reasoned" before the word risk. I feel obligated to add a modifier lest someone think I'm championing the cause of reckless abandon. I don't like to use the word "calculated" because that word implies there is no room for intuitive interpretation. Reasoned risk implies some thoughtfulness, as well as information gathering—reflected through a prism of sound judgment.

When you consider how much is dependent on a company's risk-taking propensity—new products, service excellence, delegation, creative problem-solving, communication—the case for increased performance in the risk-taking area is clear. Managers who will not take reasoned risk are about as useful in today's business environment as a parachute that opens on the second bounce. Risk-averting managers are often a source of frustration to their employees and a primary reason their companies lack the responsiveness needed to prosper, or even survive, in a world of rapid change.

Turning failure into victory

1. Keep yourself informed. By keeping yourself informed on issues relevant to your work, you will minimize the amount of your decision that needs to be intuitive.

2. Increase risk-taking propensity by practicing on smaller challenges first. Contrary to popular opinion, in business risk-taking is more an acquired skill than a personality trait.

3. Accept failure for what it really is—a learning experience. Few failures are fatal, just as few victories are final. Learn to appreciate failure. While it shouldn't be your goal, there is usually at least one valuable lesson you can learn from it.

4. Choose to take risks when the time is right. If you don't, you may be forced to take them when the time is wrong.

5. Model the behavior you expect. If you want talented and capable people around you, let them see that you value and support reasoned risk-taking.

Part 7:
Customer Service

Mess-Up No. 29

Failure to understand that exemplary customer service is no longer an option.

"In today's service-oriented economy, excellent service is more than a competitive weapon—it's a survival skill."

—Michael LeBoeuf, Ph.D.

When my daughter was younger, we went out shopping one weekend for a new telephone-answering machine. As I started to pull into the parking lot of a nationally known electronics store, she asked if we could go somewhere else. Surprised, I asked why. "Every time I go in there," she said, "they make me feel unimportant." I was surprised by her comment, because this company sells products purchased in volume to younger consumers.

As we headed to another electronics chain, one my daughter said always treated her well, I asked her to tell me more about the first company. "When I go in there," she said, "I feel like I'm invisible. It doesn't matter where I am in line, the older customers will always be taken care of first. It's like I'm not there. And no one ever seems to appreciate my business," she continued, picking up steam. "I know for a fact that I've never been thanked."

One lesson many of America's businesses—large and small—have failed to learn is that exemplary customer service is no longer an option. It's not something that a company with plans for growth can afford to overlook. Please note that I said *exemplary* service was not an option. If your service is anything less, you don't have a chance. Many companies start out with a commitment to service, but see it fall away bit by bit. It reminds me of a scene from a William Faulkner novel where a bunch of playboys are sitting in a bistro discussing business. One of the men, unfamiliar with the concept of going broke, asked how one goes bankrupt. A friend replies, "A little at a time, then all at once."

When it comes to exemplary customer care, you can get some pretty good insights from Karl Albrecht, Ron Zemke, Michael LeBoeuf, and Tom Peters—four of America's top experts on the subject. But if you're looking for some really meaty stuff with real staying power, take a look at one of America's first nationally known speakers on the topic of service, Benjamin Franklin. Here's what Franklin had to say about customers back in 1749:

> *Lay a good foundation in regard to principle: Be sure not willfully to overreach, or deceive your neighbor; but always keep in your eye the golden rule of doing as you would be done unto. Endeavor to be as much in your shop, or in whatever place your business properly lies, as possibly you can. Your presence may prevent the loss of a good customer. Be complaisant to the meanest, as well as the greatest: You are as much obliged to use good manners for a farthing, as a pound.*

> *Be not too talkative, but speak as much as is necessary to recommend your goods. If customers slight your goods, and undervalue them, endeavor to convince them of their mistake, but do not affront*

them: *do not be pert in your answers, but with patience hear, and with meekness give an answer. for if you affront in a small matter, it may possibly hinder you from a future good customer. They may think you are dear (expensive) in the articles they want; but by going to another, may find it not so, and probably may return again; but if you behave rude and affronting, there is no hope either of returning, or their future custom.*

Strive to maintain a fair character in the world: That will be the best means for advancing your credit, gaining you the most flourishing trade, and enlarging your fortune. Condescend to no mean action, but add a lustre to trade, by keeping up to the dignity of your nature.

—Milton Meltzer, *Benjamin Franklin:*
The New American

What Franklin believed in, he believed in with a passion. His beliefs, combined with his creativity, innovation, and practical wisdom, earned him the reputation as the most dangerous man in America by the crowned heads of England. His focus and commitment were frightening to those whose interests he challenged. If Franklin was alive today and practicing his common sense approach to meeting customer needs, he would be known as the most dangerous man in America. Only this time, it would be by those who tried to compete with him head-to-head in business without putting the customer first.

Turning failure into victory

Two and a half centuries later, Franklin's words about customer service still ring true. If Franklin were alive today, people would be buying his books and CDs by the boatload. In closing out this chapter, the keys to turning this Mess-Up around come to you (paraphrased) courtesy of the father of exemplary service in America, Benjamin Franklin.

1. The only firm foundation in business is one built, block by block, on customer satisfaction. Exemplary customer service requires a solid base of principle and purpose.

2. State your capabilities as honestly as possible. Exemplary customer service does not promise what it cannot deliver, nor does it promise less.

3. Treat every transaction as equal, regardless of appearances or value. Do not serve the order as much as the customer. Small customers often become bigger, more loyal ones.

4. Be available to your customers and associates. Not being around when you're needed conveys disinterest in your customers' needs.

5. Make your service noticeable by its distinction for excellence. Let your "lustre"—your added value—be visible to all who deal with you. Don't badger your customer, or haggle over price.

6. Let your service be distinguished by your patience, courtesy, kindness, sincerity, fairness, and helpfulness.

Mess-Up No. 30

Failure to teach employees that policies are general guides—not dictates to behavior.

"Rules and regulations are for the guidance of wise men and the blind observance of fools."

—Anonymous

I carry a well-worn clipping taken from a *USA Today* newspaper several years ago as a reminder of the importance of this Mess-Up. The article tells the story of a West coast man who walked into a branch of his bank and cashed a check for $100. As he left he asked the receptionist if she would validate his parking ticket. She asked if he had completed a transaction with the bank. "Yes," he said, "I cashed a check." "I'm sorry," she replied, "we don't consider cashing a check to be a transaction."

"You're kidding me," the man said with genuine surprise. "You mean if I put money in it's a transaction, but if I take it out it's not?" "That's about it," the receptionist noted. "That doesn't make any sense," the customer responded. "I'm sorry," the receptionist said dispassionately, "it's our..." When I share this story in my seminars, I leave the last word in this illustration unspoken. Without prompting, everyone always responds: "policy!"

The story continues. Dissatisfied with the receptionist's response, the man asks to see the manager. The manager listens to the man's request, and then answers by saying that it is indeed the bank's policy, and that the ticket could not be validated for a nontransaction. Thoroughly disgusted, the man proceeded to close out all of his accounts with the bank and take his business elsewhere. Why did this story make the front page of USA Today? Because he had a little more than $2 million in his accounts.

Not that unusual

Unbelievable, you say? In reality, millions of dollars are lost daily by banks and other businesses because of the blind observance of policies. Unlike the bank in this story, however, they are losing it in smaller—and more easily overlooked—amounts.

Several years ago I took my daughter to a movie at a shopping mall. As we passed a well-known national bookseller, I noticed a table out front with books reduced in price by 15 percent. I saw a book on Churchill I wanted, but decided to pick it up after the movie. When I returned two hours later, the book was still on the table, but without a sticker. Assuming I would still get the discount, I picked up the book and headed inside to browse further.

After retrieving several books from the business section, I proceeded to the line forming at the checkout counter. When my turn came, I mentioned to the clerk that the Churchill book was from the discount table, although its sticker was missing. Without looking up she answered, "Sorry, that sale is over." She keyed in the full price and started to ring up the other books. "You've got to be kidding," I said. "Who ends a sale at 4:23 in the afternoon?" "We do," she chirped. Then, in an effort to be humorous, she added, "You snooze you lose!" "No," I replied, "you guys lose." I left without making a purchase.

The more I thought about the incident, the more it bothered me. The next day I called the manager of the store to express my displeasure. After listening patiently as I told my story—a pleasant surprise—the lady responded, "I'm very sorry that occurred." Not bad, I thought. It's always nice to get an apology. She continued. "And I apologize for the inconvenience." Hey, I thought, we're making progress here! It was her third statement that came up short in my estimation. She concluded, "If my employee had only asked me, I would have authorized the reduction."

Hiding places

How does a bank lose a $2-million depositor over a 60-cent parking ticket? How does a bookstore lose a $100 purchase over a $1.27 discount? The answer to both is a failure by management to teach employees that policies are guides to behavior, not something to hide behind when you are unable or unwilling to accommodate a customer request. In both of the situations illustrated, rigid adherence to policy was a substitute for good judgment. And the problem goes much deeper than the loss of business.

One of the key elements of success in today's rapidly changing business environment is flexibility. Being able to respond quickly and effectively to customer demands requires employees who are well-trained and empowered to respond to customers' needs. An employee who has to seek out the manager in order to make a $2 decision will not be satisfied with the work. What do you suppose the impact is on employees' self-esteem if their employer does not trust them to make a $2 decision in the best interests of the customer (and the company)?

I'm not suggesting we should throw out all policies and let employees improvise. What I am saying is that we should remember that the purpose of a policy is to provide guidance in making a decision that benefits all parties if possible. A company that relies solely on blind adherence to policy loses one of its key factors in being an effective competitor: motivated employees who use good judgment and creativity in carrying out their responsibilities.

Turning failure into victory

1. Empower your employees with more than slogans. Give them a defined level of authority that fills the need to meet the customer's expectations for service. The winners in today's fast-paced market empower the person who makes first contact with customers.

2. Provide training to go along with the authority. Thoroughly define your company's expectations in terms of meeting customer needs. Define your company's values and objectives, its mission, and its purpose. This will provide a framework against which employees can base their decisions.

3. Give your employees latitude in interpreting policies based on their good judgment and their understanding of the impact of their decision on the customer's satisfaction. Let them know you trust them, but that they will be held accountable for their decisions.

4. Hire good people, train them well, and then learn to rely on their judgment. The companies that will prosper in

the future will be those uninhibited by rules and regulations that factor out the customer's needs and the employee's ability to meet them.

5. Reconsider any policy or procedure that frustrates the people who interface directly with the customer. The people responsible for carrying out a policy should be involved in its development. Give your staff "ownership" in rules that govern their work.

◻

Mess-Up No. 31

Failure to meet routinely with customers—internal and external—to discover what they really want.

> "The Japanese were wiping us (Harley-Davidson) out because they were better listeners."
>
> —Vaughn Beals, former Chairman of the
> Board, Harley-Davidson

I met a railroad engineer recently, the guy who actually drives the train. I told him that, as a boy, I had loved seeing the engineers, whistle rope in hand, leaning out the window to inspect the tracks ahead. "Actually," the man told me, "that's not what they were doing." He went on to tell me that the real reason the engineer leaned out the cab wasn't to check the tracks but to listen to his engine. "He's so close to his machine," the engineer said, "he can easily detect if something is wrong with his ears alone." It's the kind of listening companies should be doing with customers: internal and external.

Plugged in

Tales of companies who turned their businesses around by rediscovering their customers are widespread these days. When Tom Peters started touting these customer service principles in his seminars and books, managers all over the country scrambled to connect with him and other suddenly valuable business consultants. In retrospect, advising companies to consult their customers about their needs is like advising a person to take a breath. Both are essential to continued good health, and should occur often for best results!

One of my favorite stories of reconnecting with customers is the one about Harley-Davidson. Having lost substantial market share to Honda in the 80s, Harley's leadership decided to get back to basics and find out what their customers wanted (aside from engines that didn't leak oil). To get this information, Harley's CEO charged his top managers to go wherever Harley users gathered and find out what the company was doing wrong. For many, it was both an eye-opener and a culture shock. (As you might imagine, a lot of Harley users don't gather in four-star restaurants and coffee houses.) After convincing their customers of their sincerity (remember, they ignored these people for a long time), the Harley team was able to corral enough advice to make the changes that enabled Harley-Davidson to roar back in the 90s.

Meeting market needs

Although passionate about service and fully aware of the marketing wisdom in meeting needs versus creating them, I fell into the ignore-the-customer trap myself. Years ago I owned a hardware store in my hometown, and one day my sales rep stopped by with a deal I couldn't refuse. The product was called a Fert-O-Matic. The genius (I thought) of the Fert-O-Matic was that it fertilized your yard as it watered it. You just had to add the fertilizer to the handy plastic dome on top and turn that sucker on. It's lemonade time while the Fert-O-Matic does all the work. The hook was set. I was going for the bulk-pack of 24 units, complete with a four color pop-up display rack. Had I been smarter, I would have purchased one of the units, sat it on the counter, and asked my customers, "What do you think about this?"

Convinced that these babies were going to jump out the door, I set the display right by the entrance (might as well give them a head start). The popularity of the Fert-O-Matic was, to say the least, underwhelming. Not only did they not sell, they were the subject of more than a few jokes ("Hey, Mark, do you have Hammer-O-Matics?"). Nine months after I put the display in place, I still had 22 of the original 24 units. The only reason I didn't have all 24 was that my daughter received a unit for her 16th birthday and my parents got one for their 60th anniversary.

Connecting with external customers

As noted earlier, I like the use of the word "connect." What used to function as two separate units is now moving forward as one. In a hyper-competitive market like the one in which most businesses today compete, moving as one with your customers is essential. In a time when product life cycles are measured in weeks or months instead of years, that communication process must be an ongoing one.

Although there are a host of traditional ways for companies to stay in touch (surveys, surveys, surveys), I think the best approach is still to meet the customer face-to-face. Years ago as director of marketing for an electronics firm, I made more sales calls than any person on the corporate payroll, and I used these face-to-face meetings to get feedback from our customers. If I made a sales call on an engineer, I always asked the "magic wand" question. Simply put, I would ask my customer, "If you could wave a magic wand and have one new product right now, what would it be?" By asking this question, I insured a never-ending flow of ideas for future products and services. (One idea given to me by an engineer was worth millions to my company. I'll tell you about it in Mess-Up No. 32.) I think Lyndon Johnson hit the nail on the head when he said, "If you ain't listening, you ain't learning." Especially to what customers want.

Connecting with internal customers

Several years ago, the concept that managers ought to treat their employees as customers caught on in business. This was one of those BFOs (Blinding Flash of the Obvious). The original idea was that these people should be valued and appreciated as much as the real thing. Somewhere along the line, however, the idea emerged that these people might have value as consultants to the company, much as outside customers did. As a consultant and trainer, it never ceases to surprise me how many firms are blind to the customer-focused knowledge of their own employees. Every day these people come into contact with their customers. Sales reps, service coordinators, maintenance personnel, receptionists, tellers, nurses, and teachers all have frequent interaction with the people buying their products or services.

I remember sitting in a meeting at a company where a number of managers were struggling over a problem with a cumbersome order entry report that directed the efforts of four departments. A heated argument over the layout of the report had ensued, and an impasse between production, sales, purchasing, and billing resulted. After getting nowhere for nearly an hour, someone suggested bringing in staff people from each of the four departments and asking them what they thought would work. At first, the staff people were a bit intimidated about being asked for their opinion. After discussing the reports for a few minutes with their managers, they were given time to discuss it amongst themselves. In less than 15 minutes, they invited everyone back. "We think we've got a solution," their spokesperson said. And they did.

An unexpected result

The idea of involving internal and external customers in your business plans makes good sense for several reasons. The first, and most obvious, is that it's a superb way to gather timely information. Noted philosopher Francis Bacon said that knowledge is power. Timely knowledge must be like nuclear power! Another benefit of involving staff and customers is that both are motivated by the idea that their opinions are valued. I used to book a lot of business just by asking questions. I didn't realize it at the time, but listening can be a very persuasive thing to do (see Mess-Up No. 5). When you ask questions and listen—really listen—you honor the people around you. And that's a win-win situation for everyone.

Turning failure into victory

1. Listen to external customers on a routine basis. This must be as much a part of your process as billing for orders shipped. Don't rely solely on surveys—verbal or written. If you are in an area that does not normally have face-to-face contact with the customer, make arrangements with your sales department to make some calls with them.

2. At least once a week, hold a brief, informal meeting with your group. Find out what they need to get their jobs done. It may be equipment, information, or training. Whatever it is, accept responsibility for meeting that need.

3. Schedule one-on-one time with your employees. One way to do this is to take an off-site coffee break. The key is to be away from the distractions of the workplace so you can give your employee your undivided attention.

4. Build "listening blocks" into your schedule and note them on your planner. Consider it an unbreakable appointment. Studies indicate that time hassles are the primary factor in preventing contact with customers. And nothing is more frustrating to customers than suppliers too busy to listen.

5. If you use surveys, share the results. One of the biggest mistakes made in this area is asking customers—inside or out—to give their time and information

without acknowledgement. Each expression of appreciation should include a copy or a summary of the results obtained.

■

Mess-Up No. 32

Failure to understand that "hustle" is a viable strategy.

"Every morning in Africa, a gazelle wakes up knowing it must run faster than the fastest lion or be killed. Every morning a lion awakens knowing it must outrun the slowest gazelle or starve to death. It doesn't matter if you are a lion or a gazelle. When the sun comes up, you'd better be running."

—African parable

The word "hustle" can be taken in several ways. On the positive side, it means to work hard to beat the other guy to the prize. On the negative side, it implies a certain sneakiness—an attempt to get ahead by manipulation or deception. In Cincinnati, the word hustle will always be associated with Pete Rose, the would-be Hall of Fame baseball player who somehow managed to epitomize both interpretations. I prefer to think of him in terms of the positive side, the side that earned him the nickname "Charlie Hustle."

The first time I saw Pete Rose play was at old Crosley Field on the west side of Cincinnati. He was a rookie right fielder intent on leaving his mark on the game. In the first inning, he received a base on balls. Most players, after being "walked," take a leisurely stroll to first base. Not Rose. He flung his bat aside and sprinted to first base as if the outcome of the game depended on how fast he covered the distance. When the inning was over, Rose raced to his outfield position with the same intensity. Late in the game, Rose used his hustle to stretch a single into a double. He scored on the next play, a lazy single up the middle. The Reds won that day by a run, a score made possible not by skill or power, but good old-fashioned hustle.

I'm convinced the Pete Rose approach to baseball is a perfect template for success in any business. Getting there first and fast is a legitimate marketing strategy. I know. I saw it happen. It was several years ago during a sales call I made on an engineer in San Jose. Sitting in his office, I asked him what we could do to distinguish ourselves. After all, there were 600 companies worldwide that made the kind of products we did. Without hesitation he responded, "Get samples to me faster."

In much of the electronics industry, nothing happens until samples are received. It's the first step in the design process and a critical one. Purchase orders are placed only when the design is complete, and that doesn't happen until engineering can secure samples to evaluate for form, fit, and function. The engineer I was working with said it was not unusual for him to wait a month or more before receiving a requested part. "It's frustrating," he said, "because our window of opportunity is limited, too." "Get me samples fast and you'll be remembered," he said. Before I left, he asked us to sample him on a couple of parts.

On the way out of his company's headquarters that day I stopped in the lobby to phone the sample request into our home office. "Let's ship these parts by FedEx for next day delivery," I said. The next morning, I knew the parts were on the engineer's desk because he called to tell me. "You really created a stir," he said. "Is that right?" I replied. "You bet," he shot back. "No one around here ever got a sample so fast." He concluded by telling me the part had been "designed in," included as a part of his product. Several weeks later we received a purchase order worth a little more than $200,000.

What my company did that day—deliver a sample within 24 hours of the request—was unheard of in the industry. It was the equivalent of Pete Rose stretching a single into a homerun. We were so struck by the simplicity of it, that we almost missed it as a way to distinguish ourselves in the market. We eventually changed our whole approach to sampling, and made a commitment to ship *all* samples in 24 hours or less. That commitment grew into a marketing strategy and worldwide advertising campaign that led to a dramatic increase in sales. Today, many companies in the electronics industry must ship samples within 24 hours just to remain competitive.

Your company's "hustle index"

How well a company responds to the marketplace in terms of speed is a primary responsibility of management today. To see how your company rates—sleek machine or sputtering clinker—simply consider the following questions:

1. Does your company challenge time-based assumptions? Do you regularly look at your business to determine what aspects are enhanced—or detracted from—by how quickly you react and respond? If it can be measured by speed, you must consider time constraints and boundaries as nothing more than temporary obstacles.

2. Do your employees understand and appreciate the need for speed? Does your staff understand the advantages to be gained by responding faster than competitors? It's essential to keep employees informed of the dynamics of your market, and why their hustle is essential for success.

3. Does your company encourage staff to advise management of obstacles (speed bumps) to responsiveness? Do employees feel free and open to discuss anything blocking their

progress, *including* management? Meeting regularly with employees to discuss their needs in responding quickly to customer demands is a key factor in speed-to-market.

4. Do employees have enough authority to respond to customer requests? Are employees constrained by burdensome decision-making processes in the company? If the people closest to the customer cannot make decisions, there is no way the company can respond in a way that creates distinction.

5. Do employees understand the consequences of sluggishness? Do they know the survival-threatening nature of inaction? It's important for managers to raise the visibility of consequences of being slow to act.

Of all the factors affecting success in today's business environment, none is as important as speed-to-market. Companies that do well understand the impact of speed and responsiveness, and they make hustle a part—if not all—of their marketing strategy. It's a good thing to remember that being slow to respond carries the same penalty in business as it does in the jungle. You end up being someone's lunch.

Turning failure into victory

1. Make sure everyone understands his or her role in the speed-generating capacity of your company. Give high visibility to those willing to plug their energies into working with greater speed, flexibility, and efficiency.

2. Make sure everyone understands that the drive to do things quickly does not imply that any other standard—such as quality or accuracy—can be sacrificed in the process.

3. Design systems that help employees react quickly and accurately. Revise policies and procedures that compromise responsiveness. As manager, see your role as a remover of obstacles impeding speed.

4. Challenge all time-based assumptions. Do not assume that there are limitations on how fast a customer can be responded to, or how fast a product can be brought to market. Consider present time constraints as temporary—not insurmountable—obstacles.

5. Model the behavior you expect. A manager without hustle cannot guide competent and competitive employees in today's supercharged business environment.

Part 8:
Getting Results

Mess-Up No. 33

Failure to understand that placing blame is unproductive.

"Peak performers concentrate on solving problems rather than placing blame for them."

—*Charles Garfield*, Peak Performers

"Who's responsible for this?" the CEO asked angrily. The question, addressed to a group of managers seated in the boardroom of a Southwest chemical company, hung in the air like a heavy cloud. The company had just lost a large account to a rival, who just happened to be the former employer of the CEO. He was not taking it well. While the managers squirmed in their seats, the man continued, "I'm going to find out who screwed this up, and when I do, I can assure you that they'll know about it." As they left the meeting, one manager said to another, "I guess we'll all be updating resumes tonight."

Finding fault

The CEO in the previous illustration was concerned with finding the employees who had caused his company to lose an order, so as to place the blame squarely at

their feet. Instead of mobilizing his troops to identify coun-
termeasures to recover the business, he made sure that
their primary energies for the next few days would be
directed to a crisis management technique called CYA
(cover your...well, you get the picture). The problem with
this technique is that nothing good comes from it. Had
the CEO taken the approach that all failures are learning
experiences, and used it as an opportunity to identify
areas for improvement, something good could have come
of something bad.

Forget blame

Several years ago I was director of sales and marketing for a small Midwest manufacturing operation. A problem had originated with a customer who wouldn't pay a
bill. I heard through the grapevine that this company was
going to file for bankruptcy. After discussing the problem
with several other managers, I decided to attempt to recover our inventory before the filing took place. One of
the customer's employees, a supervisor in the warehouse,
had agreed to give us the inventory not paid for while the
owner was away. Because this supervisor was quitting,
he didn't mind helping out.

Everything went as we had planned. It wasn't exactly
the raid on Entebbe, but it was fairly exciting. Our sales
rep drove around to the back of the warehouse with a
van and, with the help of the warehouse supervisor, loaded
up about $45,000 worth of inventory. I felt a sense of ex-
hilaration at saving my company a considerable loss from
a bankruptcy settlement. Unfortunately, I had neglected
to learn that the inventory, unsecured by my company,
had been pledged as security to our customer's bank. So,
we not only had to return the inventory, we had to pay
the resultant court costs, too.

I remember the day I went in to tell my boss, the president and owner of the company, what had happened. Like

the men in my opening illustration, I spent the night before updating my resume. I figured at best I'd get a pretty decent chewing out, and at worst, an opportunity to see how good that resume was. When I told my boss what I had done and why, he listened without comment. When I told him what the cost to the company might be, he didn't bat an eyelash.

When I finished my story, the president looked at me and said, "Okay, that's over. Now go do something to make us some money." The effect his words had on me was momentous. I think I worked harder the next six months than I ever had. We had a record sales year and recorded higher profits than ever before. The strategy of the president of this company was a simple one. Placing blame is an exercise in futility. Rather than focus on what had been lost (his money), he chose to concentrate on building confidence and a future.

Placing blame

Resisting the chance to prove someone wrong can be difficult. It takes a great deal of maturity, not to mention foresight, to avoid blame and press on to solving the problem. The emotional impact of finding fault and placing blame can cause more damage than the problem itself. What's the cost of a demoralized work force? The benefits of placing blame are few, while the liabilities are numerous. Here are a few blame-placing negatives I picked up in a workshop years ago.

❖ Blame never affirms, it assaults.

❖ Blame never restores, it wounds.

❖ Blame never solves, it complicates.

❖ Blame never unites, it separates.

❖ Blame never smiles, it frowns.

❖ Blame never forgives, it rejects.

❖ Blame never builds, it destroys.

Don't bring me problems

During one of my seminars, a young manager told me about problems he'd encountered when he took over a new department. Managed previously by a man who found fault often, the group felt reluctant to make decisions on anything. I asked him how he had handled the situation. He told me he had gathered his staff together and told them that, effective immediately, they were not to bring him a problem unless they had developed at least one possible solution on their own. "A lot of my people were both shocked and frightened by my rule," he said. The man went on to tell me that the results in the beginning were not encouraging. "I immediately noticed a significant drop in the number of questions coming to me," he said. "I had hoped they were thinking their problems through, and were coming up with their own solutions." What he later discovered, however, was that many situations that needed answers had been placed on hold while workers worked up the courage to come see him.

The problem was solved, I learned, when the man brought his group together a second time. "Look," he said, "I'm not interested in placing blame for things that don't work. And I'm certainly not looking for perfect answers. I just don't want you to be dependent on me to get your work done." After that, the manager and his staff agreed on some ground rules for solving problems. He reassured them that they did not have to have the right answer, just a suggestion that might work. When their confidence rose and the suggestions started coming in, they were right far more often than they were wrong.

Turning failure into victory

1. Establish a framework for failure within your group. Let people know in advance that you find placing blame to be a counter-productive exercise, except in circumstances when it may be helpful in identifying growth

opportunities. Let your staff know that failure is never final, and that you are committed to exploring all options.

2. Establish ground rules for risk-taking. Tell your staff that well-thought-out ideas and solutions that come up short will not be punished or criticized, but will instead be treated as valuable learning experiences.

3. Recognize that finding fault and placing blame are, in most circumstances, an immature approach to both business and life. Real success and happiness in life does not come until this unproductive behavior is overcome.

4. Provide your staff with sufficient encouragement and information so they will know what is expected of them, and so they will believe in your leadership and themselves enough to meet those expectations.

5. Acknowledge those who have taken reasoned risk and failed as heroes. See these failures as learning opportunities. "Don't bring me anything but trouble," Charles Kettering once said, "good news weakens me!"

Mess-Up No. 34

Failure to understand the relationship between control, self-esteem, and productivity.

"Until you value yourself, you will not value your time. Until you value your time, you will not do anything with it."

—M. Scott Peck, *The Road Less Traveled:*
A New Psychology of Love,
Traditional Values and Spiritual Growth

I was scheduled to conduct a series of seminars on customer service in Chicago a few years ago. I'm always a little apprehensive about doing service programs until I meet the top executives of the company and determine their levels of commitment. Without the endorsement and sponsorship of top management, most training on this topic will have a short-lived impact, regardless of program content or presentation style.

I met on the Friday preceding the week of the programs with the company's CEO, who resided in what I like to call the "throne room." His desk was as big as a boxcar. The chairs his visitors sat in were considerably lower, leading you to suspect the legs had been shortened for special effect. The overall impression, as you sat talking to the man, was more like an audience with a king than a meeting of equals.

The CEO and I chatted for a few minutes about his company's background, when he suddenly changed the topic. "Look," he said, "I'll come right to the point. What I want you to do next week is to kick butt, and keep on kicking it until these people learn to love the customer." Needless to say, I knew I was in trouble. As a motivational tool, this man's approach rated right up there with the classic strategy of "The firings will continue until morale improves!"

The 10 half-day seminars (we wanted smaller groups) began on Monday morning as scheduled. As I stood before the first group, looking at a room full of blank faces, I thought I might be in for a long morning. I sensed an unusually high level of listener resistance, and decided to skip my "B" jokes in favor of my "A" material. No luck. No matter what I tried, no one would interact in any meaningful way. All morning, my audience shifted restlessly in their chairs, consulting their watches with annoying frequency!

At lunch, I went off on my own to a little park on the company's property. I was fairly distressed with the results of the first program, and wanted to think about possible changes for the next one. I wasn't sure how to do it, but I knew I had to avoid a recurrence of that earlier session. When the second group came into the training center, I had a whole different approach lined up for them.

Unfortunately, the earlier group must have met with these guys in the hall and conducted a mini-workshop on how to resist seminar leaders, because they were equally resistant. Late in the afternoon, we took a break. While in the rest room I overheard one of my participants comment to another, "You know, if it wasn't for that memo I received from my boss, I could be enjoying this program."

I approached the man who made the comment and, apologizing for listening in on his conversation, asked if he could tell me what the memo had said. He sheepishly advised me the memo had stated that his presence at these meetings was mandatory. I don't know what your reaction to the word mandatory is, but few people react to it positively. "Mandatory" is a classic control word that invokes all kinds of resistance in everyone from children to teenagers to adults. The control issue is a major one for managers faced with supervising workers seeking more control over their jobs.

The best job

I read an article several years ago that stated that the best job to have to ensure a long life was that of a symphony conductor. When I first read the article, I assumed the reason for a symphony conductor's long life had something to do with the aerobic nature of the work. According to the article, however, that was not the case. It seems the element of the job that leads to a long life is control. The conductor has ultimate control over his orchestra. They begin when he says to begin, they play as fast or as loud as he instructs, and they end when he says to.

While holding the baton may be an exhilarating experience (who doesn't like to be in control?), those who lead need to remember what it feels like to be on the other end. Many workers today are frustrated by the lack of control they have at their jobs. Employees who feel they must always follow someone else's lead, with no room for improvisation or creativity, experience high levels of frustration and burnout.

From riches to rags

During a program, a young manager shared with me the effect a loss of control had on her company. It seems the owner/president of the company liked to escape the winter weather. Sometime around mid-October, he would pack up and head south where he would stay until the spring thaw. Although he stayed in touch with his staff through phone conversations and monthly reports, the actual operation of the company was left in the hands of senior management. At first, these managers found his absence intimidating and tried to guess what the owner's decisions would be. Despite his absence, they still felt very much under his control.

One winter, while the president was catching rays on the beach, his managers held an off-site meeting to discuss some problems they were having. At times the session had all the appearances of a good old-fashioned free-for-all. Some managers wanted to exercise their own judgment. Others were concerned that the owner wouldn't appreciate that. By the time the meeting drew to a close, a meeting of the minds had been reached. For better or worse, the management team was going to call the shots. It was the beginning of what the woman recounting the story to me described as something special. "We really learned how to work together after that meeting," she said. "The cooperation and enthusiasm were unbelievable."

That enthusiasm, it seems, had a positive impact on overall performance. "Our sales were up 25 percent," the woman said, "and we were shipping 98 percent of our orders on time. We were really getting things done!" she said. Because people had control over the events associated with their lives and work, self-esteem had skyrocketed. The increase in self-worth led to an equal jump in productivity. In every way progress is measured, this company was growing.

By the time the spring thaw arrived, the company was looking forward to the return of the owner. They were confident that a well-deserved pat on the back would be given to them for what was obviously a job well-done. When the president returned, nothing was said for several days as he appeared to be "casing the joint." Before long, it became obvious that he was not looking for things to praise. Some even thought he seemed to be going out of his way to find something to be displeased with. When the managers were finally called together for a meeting, they were beginning to sense that a pat on the back was not on the agenda.

Nevertheless, what followed shocked everyone present. The president, legal pad in hand, proceeded to berate his staff for allowing the company to become what he called a "slipshod operation." "He went over his list and cited everything he was unhappy about," I was told. "He ripped one manager because one of his employees was sitting at his desk reading a newspaper. But the paper was an industry journal important to the guy's job," the woman said. "We were devastated," she added. According to the woman's account, things went downhill from there. The president took control once again, and the management team reverted to their old habit of waiting to be told what to do.

The lady had given me her business card, so I followed up with her several months after the program. I was told when I called that she was no longer with the company. I did get her number, however, and caught up with her later in the week. She was glad to give me a postscript to the story. "After that experience," she said, "things really got bad. We all felt worthless, and began to act like it." She went on to say that it got to the point where the owner was deciding everything. Frustrated and bored, this manager, like a number of her comanagers, gave notice and left. "I'm not making as much money," she said, "but at least I feel good about myself."

Turning failure into victory

1. Don't legislate action to employees. Communicate the outcome you expect, and then give them some latitude in deciding the best way to achieve that objective. Let them feel a sense of ownership when the outcome is achieved.

2. Teach good time-management techniques. One of the biggest robbers of self-esteem is the loss of control over the events of your life due to poor allocation of time resources.

3. Delegate! By delegating the "good stuff" to employees, you will not only motivate them by your faith in their ability to carry out the task, but by the ownership they can claim in the results achieved.

4. Energize with praise! Nothing builds the self-esteem of an employee as much as genuine praise and recognition for work well-done. Look for ways to acknowledge efforts in unique and creative ways.

5. Provide training opportunities. Training is a powerful symbol that sends the message that employees are important and a part of the future. Learning increases knowledge, which, in turn, increases self-esteem and greater control over the events of our lives.

Mess-Up No. 35

Failure to understand that the ultimate factor in success is not talent or method, but desire and effort.

"I achieved what I did because of my coaches, and my willingness to work hard."

—Sadaharu Oh, Japanese baseball player and all-time home run leader

Several years ago, tennis legend Jimmy Connors drew the attention of millions worldwide for his electrifying performance in the U.S. Open. For a few magic moments, Connors turned back the hands of time and played some of the best tennis of his career. He reached the semifinals just a few days short of his 40th birthday, a feat unmatched in professional tennis. Those of us who have grown older along with Connors vicariously enjoyed every minute of his improbable performance. What carried Connors to that moment? Was it talent, strategy, or cunning? Was it superb conditioning? While all of these played a part, none was as big a factor as Connors' intense desire (and resulting effort) to win.

All of us have witnessed at some point in time an extraordinary performance by an athlete who just seemed to will himself or herself to victory: a marathon runner who stumbles short of the finish line, but somehow rouses himself to stagger across it and win; a basketball player who, despite 40 minutes of relentless action, finds a way to rise a little higher at the end; a gymnast who injures her foot on her first vault, but despite fierce pain, somehow manages one more jump. I'm tempted to add "and wins." But winning is not the objective.

Desire and effort

Desire (effort) is a remarkable characteristic in a person. In Japan, where they actually vote on things like this, desire (*doryoku*) is considered to be one of the most important words in their culture. Sadaharu Oh, the Japanese baseball great who broke Babe Ruth's home run record, thinks effort is so important that when asked to sign his autograph he writes, *doryoku*—the Japanese word for effort. "My name means nothing," he notes. "Effort is all that matters." Indeed, desire and effort are inseparable as key ingredients for success, whether in the arena or in the office. Together they are synergistic force multipliers that enable us as individuals and businesses to exceed our capabilities.

In hiring staff, I've been successful over the years by insisting on two qualities: a teachable spirit and a willingness to do the necessary work. Whenever I deviated from these criteria, the results came up short of expectations. I once hired a young man for an entry level sales position. He was an excellent communicator, and seemed to know all the key concepts associated with our technology. He convinced me that he had a great desire to succeed. I assumed his natural talent and knowledge would carry him to immediate success. By ignoring my criteria, I had hired a man who would severely disrupt the department.

The man I hired, I'll call him Scott, turned out to be one of those people who believe they could have whatever they want by letting others do the work. Sales calls came into the office and were rotated among the various sales reps. The load could get pretty heavy, and the stress considerable. Scott had a habit of disappearing from the office on a regular basis. While the others worked, Scott always had to go somewhere to "check something." Resentment from the other workers grew to the point that they eventually came to me as a group to complain.

Scott turned out to be what I call a "creamer." The word comes from the migrant pickers in Southern California and refers to those pickers who would run ahead of others to grab the low fruit in the trees. Those who followed would have to put their ladders into the trees and climb up to get the harder-to-reach fruit. They called those who ran ahead of the others "creamers," and had a unique way of dealing with them.

Those who were caught "creaming" were brought before the others and were forced to put their feet in a concoction that would stain their feet blue. In the future, when they applied for jobs as pickers, they were asked to show their feet. If they were blue, they wouldn't be hired. Managers, more than anything else, need to make sure that the feet of their workers—and their own, too—are free of the stain of an uninspired effort.

Turning failure into victory

1. Deserve victory. Regardless of the outcome, make sure that your group deserves to win. Put the emphasis on the effort, not on the outcome. Nothing is as hollow as an undeserved victory.

2. Acknowledge and reward effort. Regardless of the outcome, reward those who put forth the effort to win. Teach people that it's the effort that brings dignity and honor to the individual and to the group.

3. Discuss the values of hard work and the satisfaction of a job well-done. It may sound old-fashioned to some, but talking with your group about the "dignity of effort" is time well-spent.

4. Give out "hustle awards" to your staff whenever they put forth great effort on an assignment. I like to give out blue dots to stick on desks for great plays, just like football coaches put on the helmets of their stars.

5. Tell success stories that emphasize the effort more than the outcome. Jimmy Connors received a hero's praise not because he won (he didn't), but because he gave everything he had to the cause.

Mess-Up No. 36

Failure to celebrate your victories.

"It is a silly game where nobody wins."

—Thomas Fuller,
chaplain extraordinary
to King Charles II

Several years ago, I went to work for a small company that would occasionally book an order for $10,000. Given the overall sales volume, I thought that was a pretty good achievement, one that should be acknowledged when it occurred. Instead, nothing happened. The order got logged in the book, and people went on with business as usual. The more I thought about it, the more I became convinced that a celebration was in order. I wasn't sure what the celebration should consist of, but I decided it was worth some thought.

One day I needed to run to the hardware store for some paint. While it was being mixed, I walked around the store to browse. I came across a big brass bell that mounted on the wall. "That's it!" I thought to myself. I bought the bell and took it back to the office. The maintenance department installed the bell while curious workers watched and wondered what I was up to.

After the bell had been installed, I called my group together and advised them that as of that moment, all orders of $10,000 or more would be celebrated. "Whoever gets the order," I said, "gets to ring the bell." As I looked around at my department, which consisted of 20 women and one man, the looks on their faces did not constitute an endorsement of the idea. "Do we have to?" one of the ladies said in a whiny voice. "No," I replied enthusiastically, "you don't have to, you GET to!" Everyone returned to their desks mumbling something about "another harebrained idea."

We had been getting an order for $10,000 or more about once every two weeks. After I installed the bell, however, we went almost six weeks without one. I thought that was kind of odd, then one day I heard a lady in the office talking on the phone to the customer. I thought I heard her mention something about an order totaling $13,000. When she got off the phone, she put her head down and started keying the order into her computer. "Renee," I said, "did you get an order of more than $10,000?" "Maybe," she replied.

I jumped up and went over to Renee and told her she should ring the bell. "Do I have to?" she asked. "Absolutely," I replied. Now Renee was no dummy. She went over to the bell, grabbed hold of the clapper, and rang the bell. The result was a sickly "ka-thunk." "That's not how you ring a bell," I said. I grabbed the chain and gave it a yank. The clang of the bell was loud enough to startle even me. Poor Renee was turning every shade of red imaginable. The rest of the department was having a group blush on Renee's behalf. "Isn't it a shame about poor Renee," they seemed to be saying.

Well, that's where we began. The next time the bell was rung, they did it a little better. The next time, better still. Before long, they were practically swinging on the chain! Excitement grew every time until one day a lady came up to me and said, "I just got an order for $20,000, can I ring it twice?" I said, "Sure, go for it!"

After that, things really began to build. One day the manager of engineering came over and said, "You guys have all the fun." "What do you mean?" I replied. "Well, every time you get an order for $10,000 you ring the bell. We do all the design work, but don't get to do anything." "Why don't you join in?" I said. He went out and bought kazoos. Whenever the bell rang in sales, 12 engineers pulled out kazoos and joined the celebration.

It wasn't long after that the production manager stopped by. "You guys have all the fun," he said. "Don't give me that," I replied. "Join in!" He went out and bought noise makers that make a sound like a horde of locusts. Whenever the bell rang in sales, an explosion of noise would erupt in the plant. You should have been there the first time we got an order for $100,000! It was absolute bedlam. But it was more than that. It was instant communication. Whenever I walked through the plant and we had not rung the bell recently, they wanted to know how things were going. "Is there anything we can do?" was an often-heard question.

Celebrating victories is important for a number of reasons. First, and most important, it just feels good. When we invest ourselves in that kind of enthusiasm, we get an opportunity to be kids again, if only for a few minutes. Not only that, these kinds of physical and emotional outbursts cause the body to release endorphins, nature's "feel good" hormone. This provides something that is often sorely needed in most offices today—a release from stress. By celebrating victories, managers are able to let their employees know what they consider to be of value. Bells can be rung for reasons other than booking big orders.

So when do we stop?

I was walking through a company's offices recently and saw a sign on the way that read: "There is no finish line." I asked the lady I was with about it, and she advised me that it was the corporate motto. "We don't want anyone getting fat, dumb, and happy," she said, "so we tell everyone there's no stopping point." I didn't say it, but I can't think of anything drearier than working in a company where opportunities are not provided to get a breather and celebrate your success.

Turning failure into victory

1. Celebrate to demonstrate values. Celebrations are how managers let employees know what is important. Meet with your department and get their feedback on what sort of things they feel are worthy of a celebration.

2. Make celebrations spontaneous! Everyone likes a surprise. Look for things to celebrate that might otherwise go unnoticed, and do it when least expected.

3. Make celebrations meaningful. Set objectives that require effort to reach, then celebrate their achievement. One company I know celebrated reaching a tough sales goal by giving each employee a bottle of champagne with a label that stated the employee's name and his or her achievement.

4. Be creative in how you celebrate. Make the unpredictability of the reward part of the celebration. I know one manager who hired a stretch limo to take his entire department to lunch...at McDonald's.

5. Use celebrations to raise energy. I know a manager who likes to celebrate the completion of tasks that are particularly difficult. He holds a celebration each year, for example, after all of the previous year's orders have been pulled and moved into storage. This is a job everyone hates, but the party restores everyone's spirit.

Mess-Up No. 37

Failure to understand that all organizations are political.

"Those who are too smart to engage in office politics are punished by being governed by those who are dumber."

—Plato

I was being interviewed for a position that, at the time, would have provided my first management opportunity. The interview had gone well, and I thought I had a good chance of landing the job. As we were wrapping up, the personnel manager said he had one last question. "Do you engage in office politics?" he asked. "Piece of cake," I thought to myself, seeing this as a set-up question. I assured him, in the best "above-it-all" tone I could muster, that I thought office politics were a disruptive factor in business and that no, I wouldn't stoop to such practices. He thanked me for my time, and concluded the interview.

Several days later I received a note in the mail thanking me for my interest, and advising that the position had been filled. Disappointed, I decided to get in touch with my interviewer to see why I had not been selected. When I called, the man was receptive to my inquiry, telling me it had come down to me and one other person. "Neck and neck all the way," he said. I asked why the other person had gotten the nod. "To tell you the truth," he said, "we were a little concerned about your response to the question on office politics. We thought your answer showed a bit of naiveté."

Of all the things I thought might have worked against me in that interview, taking the high road on the issue of office politics was not one. After I hung up, I thought to myself, "If they want a bunch of back-stabbing managers, they can hire someone else." It never occurred to me, at least not until much later, that the question asked was not "Do you support backstabbing?" but simply, "Do you *engage* in office politics?"

Politics or bust!

It's a measure of just how cynical we've become that the word "politics" carries so many negative connotations. When you insert the word "office" in front of it, the picture gets even murkier. Phrases like "back-biting" and "turf wars" immediately come to mind. Many people go through life hoping they'll one day find the perfect company where teamwork and cooperation reign supreme. Well, I have good news and bad news. The bad news is that the perfect company does not exist. The good news is that this doesn't have to be a problem.

The best managers fully understand and accept the fact that all organizations—companies, schools, churches, associations—are political. As Jean Hollands, author of

Same Game, Different Rules, notes, "The person who says 'I'm not political' is in great danger." "Only the fittest will survive," she says, "and the fittest will be the ones who understand their office's politics."

Savvy managers understand both the assets and liabilities of their company's political system. They have a mental picture of the system, and have both an offensive and defensive strategy. The offensive strategy helps them secure the things they want and need for their departments and careers. The defensive strategy helps them hang onto resources or power that others may try to snatch away.

Office politics, at its worst, can be a disruptive force in both the culture and the performance of an organization. On the other hand, a strong case can be made that a company free of "office politics" might not function as well. That, by the way, was the point made (obliquely) by the personnel manager I mentioned earlier. The most successful managers are those who recognize that all organizations are political, and use that understanding to their benefit.

Playing the game

Politics in business arose for the same reasons it did in the rest of our lives: limited resources had to be distributed, and a system to govern that distribution had to be devised. When a sales manager asks a production manager for a faster shipment, he's really asking that manager for a limited resource: time. The production manager knows that if the request is agreed to, it will cause her some difficulties in other areas. She knows it would be "bad politics" to blow the sales manager's request off, so she plays the game. "Tell you what I'll do," she says, knowing he has access to top management. "You tell the people up front that I need some new scales, and I'll push your order through." "Deal," the sales manager says. His order ships the next day.

The start of a promising political career is the decision to get in the game. For managers, this decision should be a "no brainer." One of the biggest mistakes managers make is to choose to stay out of office politics. By doing so, they remove themselves from the process that facilitates action throughout the organization. This system of government is actually critical to the organization's primary internal function: The allocation and movement of resources.

Poll the voters

No good politician makes any commitments until he or she knows which way the political wind is blowing. Most accomplish this through the use of polls, or by exposing themselves to their constituency for one-on-one feedback. It might come as a surprise, but the best politicians are much better at listening than they are talking. Many attribute Bill Clinton's success to his extraordinary listening skills. People who have spoken to the former president often come away with the same feeling: I had his full attention. Clinton understood the need to go where the voters were, and *really listen* to them. Be alert to listening opportunities that enable you to know what issues are on the minds of employees throughout your company.

Build a constituency

No politician worth his coattails would fail to develop a loyal base of support, especially with today's emphasis on participative management. The savvy manager understands that real power is granted more than given, so he is concerned with building a base of support for his candidacy. He does this the same way all politicians do it. He discovers the wants and needs of other people—especially those in key positions—and develops ways to help meet them.

Get "elected!"

Good politicians (and managers) understand that the object of the game is to get people to "vote" for them (or their ideas). A typical day for a manager consists of somewhere between 150 to 300 informational transactions. Many of these transactions are attempts to persuade someone to give the manager something he or she wants, or to prevent losing something he or she has. These transactions are, in essence, mini-elections. Winning as many of these as possible is what success in business is all about.

Advertise

Good politicians are outstanding at keeping others informed of their successes. A good manager does no less. He makes sure that those in positions of power know of his contributions. Many managers rely solely on word-of-mouth promotion to get the job done. Others act like an advertising agency, making regular PR releases. However you choose to accomplish it, make sure you blow your own horn. Don't make the mistake of thinking your work will speak for itself. It just doesn't work that way.

There are some who believe that office politics, in this age of communication and participative management, are less of a factor than before. However, studies show that office politics are actually needed more in a business environment that functions more like a democracy. Years ago when autocratic management was the rule, management functioned more like a dictatorship. Today, real diplomacy is needed to get things done. That's when politicians in business are at their best.

Turning failure into victory

1. Stay abreast of the information circulating on the office grapevine. Although the information is often not based in fact (many of those keeping the rumor mill

running have political agendas of their own), the politically astute manager needs to know what the constituency is talking about.

2. Build internal networks. Politicians like to call these "coalitions." In any language, they are essential to keeping informed and to establishing useful alliances in other areas. Networks work best when they are mutually beneficial, so look for opportunities to create reciprocal value.

3. Look like the best candidate. In politics, the key is to get elected, no matter what the race. The reason most political candidates wear nice suits and style their hair is because appearance matters. See Mess-Up No. 21 on the importance of a manager's personal style.

4. Know your constituency. Take the time to know what the interests are of the people with whom you want to connect. Know as much about them personally as you can without invading their privacy. Know what their hopes and aspirations are as well, and look for ways to support their efforts.

5. Blow your own horn. Part of the political process involves letting others know about your success.

◻

Mess-Up No. 38

Failure to hold the mediocre performer accountable.

"Every mediocre employee we hang onto is one our competition doesn't have to worry about accidentally hiring."

—Anonymous worker sarcasm

In the army, they're called a ROADY (retired on active duty). It's a derogatory term that refers to a soldier just passing the time and doing the minimum necessary to get to retirement. The concept, however, is not unique to the military. Companies worldwide are suffering the effects of employees engaged in the same practice. The only difference is that the "retirement age" has a much wider range. ROADYs in business can be 30-year employees, or a recent hire. They are part of a vast multitude (every company has at least one) of adequate, but uninspired, employees who have a penchant for getting little done.

It's been said that the two biggest obstacles a company has to overcome are a lack of capital and mediocre employees. Fortune Magazine, in an article detailing why many executives fail, cited an unwillingness to fix people problems as a key factor. The effect of failing to deal with an employee who exhibits sustained mediocrity can be enormous. Not only does it have a direct impact on the company's bottom line, it can become a cancer within the company eating away at everything from employee morale to the service provided customers. Of all the Mess-Ups a manager can commit, tolerating poor performance may be one of the worst.

The messages are loud and clear

Perhaps the most damaging aspect of accommodating mediocre performance is the messages it sends. To employees, it communicates the idea that less than your best is acceptable. Because mediocre employees lack enthusiasm and commitment to solve problems, the message to customers is that service is a low priority. And as good workers get discouraged and find better opportunities, the message sent to the marketplace (and future recruits) is that you can't hang on to your best people. These messages can have only one effect: The loss of competitive edge. And that's a message the competition is sure to pick up on.

Whenever I'm working one-on-one with employees, I often ask this question: If you had a magic wand and could wave it over your company and change one thing, what would it be? Not surprisingly, the answer usually involves an individual. What is surprising, however, is how often that person is an underachieving coworker. I was discussing just such a problem recently with a worker I'll call Mandy. "I don't know why it is," the woman told me, "but Kelly (not his real name) over there gets away with murder." "In what way?" I asked. "There are eleven of us in this department that bust our tails every day," she said. "But he comes in late, does little work—sometimes he even sleeps at his desk—and always has a reason for leaving early." "How long has he been here?" I asked. "Fifteen years," she replied. "You know the worst part?" she asked. "We all get the same raises."

As I continued my dialog with Mandy, I learned just how deep-rooted her resentment—and that of her productive coworkers—was. Not surprisingly, it wasn't all directed toward Kelly, who she acknowledged to be an otherwise agreeable person. Most of her resentment was directed toward managers who appeared indifferent to the problem. "So you've discussed this with your boss?" I asked Mandy. "Yep," she answered curtly. "And what was her response," I asked. Mandy replied, "She told me her hands were tied and that we needed to focus on more important things." "And what was your reply?" I inquired. "I did what she said," Mandy replied, "and focused on more important things. I sent out my resume."

Why mediocrity is tolerated

It's a topic of heated debate from lunchrooms to boardrooms: Why do otherwise competent managers fail to deal with the mediocre employee? It's a discussion that grows even more strident when good employees see mediocre workers receiving pay increases that match or exceed their own. It's astonishing how often managers put off dealing with the problem. Here's my shortlist of possible reasons:

The Too-Many-Fires Factor. The comment from the manager above that "we need to focus on more important things" is not an uncommon statement. With companies operating at reduced manpower levels, dealing with mediocrity may seem like a problem that can be put off. After all, something is better than nothing when you're swamped, right? By the way, there's a direct correlation between mediocrity and the number of fires to be put out.

The Replacement Cost Factor. Every manager knows how difficult and time consuming it is to go through the process of hiring a new employee. Recruitment-weary managers dread the process of running ads, soliciting resumes, and conducting interviews. Besides, in a shrinking job market, the person hired might not even be an improvement. Maybe Kelly isn't that bad after all?

The Grandfather Factor. Sometimes, when legislation is passed, certain individuals are exempted because they were already engaged in the process to be altered. The legal term for the exemption is called a Grandfather Clause. In some cases, mediocre performers have been "grandfathered" in and managers, who inherit the problem, feel detached from the responsibility to correct it.

The Confrontation Factor. Many managers make the mistake of falling into the "go along to get along" trap. They are unwilling to ask for more in terms of output and effort because they don't want to deal with the stress of a possible negative reaction. Mediocre employees, by the way, are counting on this.

The Reprisal Factor. I know a company that tolerated a mediocre manager for years for fear that terminating him would lead to a lawsuit. In many cases, this is a legitimate concern as companies are often unsure of what the courts might do with employees who are part of a protected class. The best defense against this type of scenario can be summed up in one word: Documentation.

The Loyalty Factor. Many managers fail to deal with the mediocre employee out of blind loyalty. Perhaps they hired the person, or have a long "history" together. Regardless, there's reluctance on the part of the manager to deal with the underachiever for fear it might be seen as an act of betrayal. This type of loyalty is misplaced, however, because it's already been compromised by a less-than loyal effort from the poor worker.

The Culture Factor. An organization's willingness to tolerate mediocrity is often the result of a culture that does not require more. A company's standard of excellence is always set at the lowest level of performance tolerated on an ongoing basis.

The Attrition Factor. I used to have a theory that if I could turn the radio in my car up louder than the noise the motor was making, I might be able to postpone having to deal with the problem. Many managers approach the problem of mediocrity in similar fashion, especially if the source of their problem is close to retirement. After all, they'll be out of here in a year or so, right?

The Compensation Factor. Failure to deal with the underachiever is often facilitated by the presence of other employees working at a higher level of accomplishment. Managers cynically rely on the character and effort of their star workers to compensate for the shortfall of poor performers. But there's a fine line between hero and martyr, and good workers grow weary of making up the difference.

The Scarlet Letter

Addressing the issue of mediocre performance is a multi-stage process with the first stage being an honest appraisal. My friend Rob Snyder, the executive director of a corporate learning center in Northern Kentucky, warns, "Don't allow the status quo to affect your thinking on what's right." Rob warns against setting the standard too low based on where the organization has been allowed to drift.

The second involves letting the organization know that a poor effort will not be tolerated. This is not a threat, but a statement that the company wants to take its performance to another level in order to insure its viability and long term success. Although it should be obvious, it may be necessary to emphasize the importance of individual performance to the overall success of the company. Remind employees that the company's future is linked to its ability to compete, and that its competitive edge is the sum-total of everyone's effort.

The next stage is to inform mediocre performers, as productively as possible, that they will no longer be able to "run under the radar," that they will be held accountable for their work. Expect some difficulty once you start talking about the "A" (accountability) word with an underachiever. Their first reaction will be resentment followed quickly by a heightened state of anxiety and vulnerability. They will know that their work is being monitored, and that their efforts have to improve.

The last stage is to provide underachievers with the encouragement and direction needed to bring them back "into the fold." Accountability means little if specific objectives aren't communicated and logged in writing. Establish well-defined objectives, laying out the steps that must be taken (and when) to accomplish each. Meet with them on a regular basis to provide feedback on their performance relative to your expectations. There should be no surprises if things fail to work out. Years of bad habits may take time to reverse, but it can be done.

If all else fails

Abraham Lincoln was continually frustrated by his inability to find good generals during the Civil War. He appointed many men to positions of leadership, only to find that they were reluctant to take action. One such general was George McClelland. Lincoln tried his best to get McClelland to act, one time sending him a terse message, "You must attack!" When McClelland refused to respond, Lincoln replaced him with Ulysses S. Grant. The rest, as they say, is history. When all else fails, managers must have the courage to make the tough call. Great battles are not won with mediocre soldiers.

Turning failure into victory

1. Do your homework. Ask yourself, "Was there ever a time when this person was a good performer? If the answer is yes, try to identify what might have caused the change. There can be a variety of reasons why a person's performance might deteriorate. Be sure that the problem is not one of poor supervision or a lack of resources.

2. Have a frank conversation. This can be an affirming meeting (*"I know you have the talent to do better..."*) or an intervention (*"It's obvious to me that you're not..."*) depending on the personality of the person and level of mediocrity you are dealing with. But it must lay out on the table the central issue: The employee is coming up short in their performance. Do not sugarcoat the problem.

3. Let them know how it makes you (and others) feel. Although no manager has the right to mess with an employee's self-image, they do have the right to express his or her feelings about a situation. Here's an example: "When you fail to complete the work you're given and someone else has to take up the slack, it makes them feel they are being taken advantage of." Let them know how frustrating and tiresome it is to have to cover for their lack of effort.

4. Create a performance improvement plan. In turning around the effort of the underachiever, it's important to have actionable steps in writing that need to be

taken. Set specific and measurable goals, with direction for achieving them. An incremental strategy may be needed at the beginning, but eventually the worker needs to know that they must consistently perform at a higher level. Have the employee sign and date the plan, then give them a copy. Review it regularly with the worker over the first ninety days of recovery.

5. Have the courage to make the tough call. As noted, many managers are reluctant to terminate a worker for fear of getting sued. Practice due diligence in documenting the employee's performance. There should be no surprises at the end of the road. Then, if the worker fails to respond to calls to improve, follow Lincoln's example.

Part 9:
General Management

Mess-Up No. 39

Failure to understand that all managers are growth leaders.

"Here's the 21st century challenge: How quickly can you ramp up, re-tool yourself, and produce results that add major value?"

—Price Pritchett,
author and management theorist

One of the great things about a public workshop is the variety of companies and industries represented. As a result, I usually begin with this question: What do you think the primary purpose of a business is? The answers received are useful in getting a feel for where the audience is relative to the function of management. Not surprisingly, most of the answers shouted out are numbers driven: "Make money!" "Create wealth!" "Turn a profit!" "It all comes down to the green stuff," a participant once said.

When I asked the question in a recent program, one manager sheepishly inquired, "Doesn't it all begin with the customer?" "Yes," I said, "it all begins—*and ends*—with the client." The most important function of any company is to create and retain customers. The amount of money it makes is simply a measurement of how good they are at doing that. It's an important concept, because it defines the primary responsibility of management: Creating an environment in which employees are equipped, empowered, and self-motivated to identify and meet customer needs. In short, the primary purpose of a manager is to be a growth leader.

Growing organically

During the 1990s, growth in many businesses was driven largely by trades, mergers, and acquisitions. After the corporate upheaval of 2000, and the legislation (Sarbanes-Oxley) it spawned, companies began to redirect their attention to organic growth as the key to building business. Organic growth, by definition, is the growth a company achieves after all "other things" (trades, acquisitions, and so on) have been factored out. It's the growth that occurs internally when a company maximizes its core competencies and creates sustainable (and profitable) performance. Companies wishing to drive this number need managers who understand their roles as growth leaders.

Barriers ahead

Although organic growth is the lifeblood of any organization, there's no shortage of obstacles—internal and external—to block its occurrence. Companies that generate high levels of organic growth have managers who are skilled at identifying and removing these barriers. Typical external constraints can be customer driven (quixotic demand, shifting loyalties), market driven (techno trends, short product life cycles), or competitor driven (increased outsourcing, predator pricing). Although a manager's ability to impact these issues may be limited by the scope of his or her responsibilities, internal constraints are a different matter.

Internal barriers to growth can be generated by a variety of factors. Some are erected by the culture of the company itself. If a company is conservative and has a less-than-tolerant attitude toward risk and failure, this is an obstacle to growth. Many internal obstacles are the result of a company's management style. Are employees empowered or controlled? Is information made available to everyone, or restricted to a few? Are leaders listening to customers and staff? Are they willing to invest in new ideas and processes, or does it seek to protect "sunk costs?" The good news is that these are obstacles that every manager has an opportunity to address on some level.

Enter the growth manager

As noted, a key factor in generating organic growth is the organizations' ability to surmount the obstacles and barriers that pop up. This requires managers who understand their role in the growth process. Here are a few key traits of those that do:

- **Growth leaders are problem-solvers.** They understand that problem-solving is the fundamental instrument of management for responding to threats and opportunities. The ability to identify current and potential problems and to make sound, timely decisions will be the principle force driving the growth of the business in the 21st century.

- **Growth leaders are powerful listeners.** Significant growth can be achieved by developing deeper relationships with customers. To accelerate the process, managers must find opportunities to hear what they have to say, an area in which few companies really excel. Don't forget internal customers (employees).

- **Growth leaders connect with customers.** A key component of organic growth is having the right information in hand regarding current customer needs, wants, and desires. Although most executives agree this is important, a recent survey showed that less than 20 percent thought their companies were doing a good job at it. Not surprisingly, research shows this to be the number-one reason companies have trouble sustaining organic growth.

❖ **Growth leaders champion, drive innovation.** Most organic growth occurs when companies find new customers, or discover ways to get more from existing ones. Another important source of growth, however, is driven by imagination and innovation: Developing new products, and finding new applications (uses, markets, and so on) for existing ones. Organic growth is facilitated in this area by managers who encourage inquisitiveness, support risk-taking, and applaud out-of-the-box thinking.

❖ **Growth leaders are powerful (accelerated) learners.** In the last decade, information and knowledge have replaced labor and capital as primary growth generating assets. One of the keys to organic growth is the degree to which managers are able to "learn, unlearn, and relearn." The future belongs to the *learning*, not the learned.

❖ **Growth leaders hustle.** The old adage that "whoever gets there first with a possible solution usually wins" has never been more relevant. A company's celerity—its quickness and flexibility—is a key factor in its ability to spot and respond to changes, threats, and opportunities. Speed-to-market (shorter product-development cycles) and customer responsiveness are key factors.

Turning failure into victory

There are many facets to being a growth manager, many of which are covered throughout this book. There are five, however, worth mentioning:

1. Strong customer focus. Connect with customers on a regular basis to gain deeper insights into their needs. Develop a clear understanding not only of where they are, but where they hope to go in the near future.

2. Protect the "flock." Looking for new business is important, but don't leave what you have exposed. Look for ways to add value to your current customer base. The best way to neutralize the "wolf" is to out-serve it.

3. Hold everyone accountable. Talk to your team in terms of outcome (growth), not tasks (duties). Make sure they understand the direct impact of their performance on the company's bottom line. Reward creativity and innovation.

4. Check often for obstacles. Conduct routine audits to see what barriers—internal and external—may have popped up to block growth opportunities. While you're at it, look for personal barriers (bias, risk aversion, and so on) too.

5. Focus on your purpose. Remember, the primary purpose of a business is to create and retain customers. The primary responsibility of a manager is to facilitate that process by creating an organization geared to driving growth.

Mess-Up No. 40

Failure to understand the importance of a performance appraisal.

"Evaluation is a time for accounting; for comparing actions with consequences; for detecting flaws and making improvements; for planting the seeds of future challenge."

—Don Koberg and Jim Banall,
*The Universal Traveler: A Soft-Systems
Guidebook to Creativity, Problem Solving and
the Process of Design*

"Have you completed your appraisals yet?" If there's one sentence guaranteed to elicit groans from the majority of managers, it must surely be this one. We hear it with regularity, because the task—evaluating the performance of workers—is the one most managers dread. One manager told me he would rather take a beating than do a performance evaluation. Another described it as her annual trip to purgatory! If the managers feel this way, can you imagine how those being evaluated must feel?

Through the years, I've been exposed to some amazing stories about the process of evaluating employees. I remember a lady who approached me during a seminar on the West coast to tell me about a new strategy her company's president had initiated. "Our president thought we were getting bogged down in the process," the lady said, "so he implemented a policy that all appraisals would consist of just one word."

I was more than a little surprised at this approach, so I asked the lady how this process worked. "Well," she answered, "once a year we go into a little conference room with our manager and chat for a while. Then the manager slides a piece of paper across the table with one word written on it that describes the behavior they think you need to work on." It was all I could do to keep from asking what word she had been given. Reading my mind she said, "Plodding. They think I need to make decisions more quickly." I told her I had heard a lot of unusual stories, but that this one topped the list!

No respect

Performance appraisals have been getting the short end of the stick for years. Many managers and supervisors approach this task as a necessary evil, instead of the great motivational opportunity it is. A performance appraisal may be the single most important time a manager will spend with an employee all year. For one thing, it may be the one time the worker has his or her boss's undivided attention. This one-on-one session is chock full of symbolism for the person receiving the appraisal. The amount of time and effort put into this review by the manager will send a loud and clear message to the employee.

Although reasons abound as to why performance appraisals come up short, a lack of preparation has to be a significant factor. With people being asked to do more and more in understaffed offices and plants, an employee appraisal frequently feels like something that can be postponed in favor of "important things." Following this approach is one way to ensure that you continue to be understaffed!

A successful performance review is created before the interview ever begins. Proper preparation insures that all the details are properly thought out and that possible legal and ethical problems will be avoided. Prior to the interview, it's a good idea to review the form you will use in its entirety. While you're at it, give a copy (unexecuted) to your employee for review as well. That way there will be no surprises—an excellent theme for every appraisal. If anything comes up during an annual (or semi-annual) appraisal that catches employees by surprise, the manager has not been doing his or her job the rest of the year.

In preparing for an appraisal, I like to go off-site for a couple of hours where I know I won't be interrupted. When I give the appraisal, I will tell my employee that he or she had my undivided attention as I reviewed his or her performance. That's a critical first step in the process, one that will send employees a message that they are important, and that I value the process enough to give it my best effort. If I think the evaluation is important, they will, too. If I give the impression that it's an imposition and speak about it disparagingly, their view of its value and importance will track those feelings accordingly.

As I put the appraisal together, I try to take care to keep the topic areas separate. I don't like appraisal forms that ask you to rate people on a scale of one to five. They're too easy to blow through without any real thought. The better forms to use are those that identify an area—such as cooperation—and provide room for the manager to write a sentence or two describing the employee's work in that category. Comments—especially negative ones— should be reinforced with examples.

Despite the bad reputations performance appraisals have, they are still desired by workers. Former mayor of New York Ed Koch used to like to ask reporters at his news conferences, "How am I doing?" Employees need an answer to this question, too. They want legitimate, carefully considered feedback on their efforts—correction if needed; a pat on the back if deserved. With few exceptions, performance appraisals are the most motivating experience a supervisor will have with workers. Making sure that the experience is *positively* motivating is what good management is all about.

Turning failure into victory

1. Value the appraisal process. Recognize that the performance appraisal is the most important time you will spend—one on one—with your employees. Tell your staff you value the process and will give it your best effort.

2. Make sure both you and your employees are familiar with the forms that will be used. Tell employees that they will have ample opportunity to share their opinions and feelings as well.

3. Make sure the area you conduct the interview in is comfortable and appropriate for the situation. Take care to avoid places associated with unpleasant circumstances.

4. Don't withhold criticism. Nobody likes to receive criticism, but if deserved, it must be given. When criticism is necessary, be clear and specific, using examples to support your view. Be sympathetic and understanding, but firm.

5. Be aware of your employees' needs and expectations. Unless you finish up with some meaningful objectives and challenges, the process will have come up short of its intended purpose of providing a path toward success.

Mess-Up No. 41

Failure to recognize the penny-wise-and-pound-foolish nature of micromanagement.

"The best executive is the one who has sense enough to pick good men to do what he wants done, and self-restraint enough to keep from meddling with them while they do it."

—Theodore Roosevelt

I was going through my e-mails recently when I came across one from a friend I had worked with a few years before. The note surprised me, because it had a resume attached and a request to refer him to any company I might know of looking for someone with his skills. When I had spoken with him last, he was excited about joining a company many considered one of the hottest career opportunities in town. Knowing what a stable person he was, it struck me as odd that he would be looking again in less than two years.

Several days later I received a call from Jim, and we agreed to meet for lunch. "I was surprised to receive your letter," I commented. "I thought you were pretty happy in your job."

"I thought this company was going to be the one I'd retire with," he said.

"I take it things didn't go as you'd hoped," I replied.

"Well, it wasn't bad for the first six months, but things went downhill after that." He then proceeded to tell me his story.

It seems my friend had been hired to manage the engineering department of a telecommunications company. Started as a little "ma and pa" operation, they had introduced a product that took off like a rocket. In just a few years, the company had grown from a dozen employees to more than 100. The problem, it seems, is that the founders of the company had a hard time letting go of the day-to-day details. Although the company had invested heavily in top notch individuals, it kept their hands tied by micromanaging every detail of the business.

"It was ridiculous," my friend said. "I'd be ready to release a project to production, and I'd have to get the owners to sign off on some meaningless detail. When I'd go to the office of one of the owner's, I'd usually have to stand in line behind several other department heads that were there for the same reason. I hated to waste time standing around waiting my turn, but I knew if I left and came back the line would just be longer."

"What was this doing to business?" I asked, thinking about their rapid growth. "Well," my friend replied, "we continued to grow but our response time kept getting longer and longer. Our sales manager really blew his stack one day when he discovered a large order had not been shipped as promised. When he went back to the production manager to complain, he found out that the raw materials had never been ordered. When he asked why, the production manager told him the president was holding the purchase request."

"Why would he do that?" I asked.

"He thought he might be able to get a better deal, so he asked the purchasing manager to leave the requisition with him. Unfortunately, his desk was buried with similar projects and this one just got lost. So did the order."

"What happened to you?" I asked. "Well, as I mentioned before, the man had to approve every little detail. To give you an idea of how bad it was, he wanted to read over any letters sent to customers before they were mailed. The man was more worried about a typo than he was about getting parts out the door. I had engineers at other companies calling me every day wanting to know where their prints or designs were. One day I suddenly realized that I wasn't the manager of this department. Despite two degrees and a pretty good track record at three other companies, I was doing the job of an entry level designer. I couldn't stand having my every move questioned anymore, so I quit."

Micromanagement

What frustrated my friend, and ultimately led to his decision to resign his position was the president's desire to control every detail of the business. It wasn't that the president was a bad person; he just had difficulty in trusting others to do the job as well as he thought he did. Instead of investing himself in the training of other workers and providing them with the information they needed to do their jobs, he created a cult of dependency on him. Ironically, he considered himself a good delegator. While he might have been good at delegating tasks, he was not good at delegating decision-making.

Micromanagement, the process of controlling every detail and decision needed to run a business or department, runs contrary to the most widely accepted management style in use today: participative. Instead of involving workers in the process, micromanagement forces the worker to stand in line and wait for a benevolent handout from the boss. In the process, a number of negatives befall the business. Here are some of the negatives associated with this management style:

❖ It compromises the efficiency and productivity of the department.

❖ It takes away the workers' pride of ownership in their work.

❖ It undermines the responsiveness and service of a company.

❖ It fosters an environment of distrust and insecurity.

❖ It robs the employee of self-esteem and job satisfaction.

❖ It contributes to a culture of fear.

In its best form, micromanagement is an impediment to productivity. At its worst it can be picky, arbitrary, and habit forming.

Turning failure into victory

Making the transformation from micromanagement to participative management first requires a change of spirit. It will require the manager to make the transformation from a style that emphasizes excessive control to one that trusts others to carry out their assignments based on their own talents and good judgment. Having committed to making that change, here are a few steps needed to see it through.

1. Encourage employees to take responsibility. Reward them for making decisions that are within the goals and objectives of the organization.

2. Provide the resources people need to do the job, and then hold them accountable for the outcomes. These resources include time, money, training, and access to key people for needed information. One of the ways micromanagers hang on to control is by hanging on to resources.

3. Establish bonds of trust with employees. Let them know that you're comfortable with their judgment, and encourage them to exercise it on matters in their area.

4. Implement a culture that empowers others to make decisions. Provide the information and training needed for people to make good and resourceful decisions. Resist the temptation to second guess every move.

5. Resist looking over the shoulder of competent employees and robbing them of the satisfaction of their jobs. Give employees an opportunity to demonstrate their dependability and resourcefulness. Be available, but don't hover.

Mess-Up No. 42

Failure to understand that part of a manager's responsibility is to make the job fun.

"The American workplace is finally discovering what humor practitioners have known all along: laughter is good business!"

—Liz Curtis Higgs, humorist and writer

I was working with a company recently when I heard the president on the intercom inviting everyone to go outside for a dedication ceremony for their new flag pole. I was a little surprised, but followed everyone else outside for the ceremony. We recited the Pledge of Allegiance, and then a young high school student played "The Star Spangled Banner" on his trumpet. Afterwards, we were each given a red, white, and blue Popsicle. The whole affair lasted 15 minutes, but everyone returned to their jobs laughing and energized by the surprise. Later, when I asked one of the managers about the ceremony, he responded, "Oh, something like that happens every week." I asked him why. "To have fun!" he responded with laughter.

Fun in the workplace

It shouldn't come as a surprise that workers consistently list having fun as one of the requirements for a satisfying job. According to recent surveys, however, few of us are achieving this. An *Industry Week* poll reveals that 63 percent of us find our work anything but fun. A number of people referred to their work as a "prison." *USA Today* reports that workplaces in America are in considerable danger of becoming "terminally serious."

The simple fact is, we've factored fun right out of the workplace. As a result, productivity, morale, and even profits have suffered. People are looking forward to going to work less and less, and with good reason. Barbara Mackoff, author of *What Mona Lisa Knew*, says work has never been such serious business. "All the more reason," she writes, "to bring a sense of pleasure to the workplace."

Are we having fun yet?

Making work fun isn't all about laughter and surprises. According to most studies on what it takes to make jobs fun, the greatest factor cited is teamwork. Groups that come together as a team in the pursuit of common objectives enjoy themselves more than those who pursue individual agendas. I was privileged several years ago to manage a group of people I consider to be the best example of what a team really is. The camaraderie, effort, and focus of this group were outstanding. In addition, there was a liberal amount of laughter and fun in the daily affairs of the group. This sense of fun came across on the phones as well. More than one customer commented on the friendliness and enthusiasm of the staff. All this despite the demanding and stressful nature of the work.

He put the fun back

When Rick Pitino accepted the head coaching job at the University of Kentucky in 1989, he accepted a position slated to be anything but fun. Racked by scandal and NCAA sanctions, Pitino's team was a bunch of "leftovers" who believed, if anything, things would get worse. A master motivator, Pitino quickly put the fun back into the game for the Wildcats. His conditioning regimens were demanding. His practices were long and hard. His encouragement and support were neverending. The emphasis was always on the team. Pitino's 1992 team, a rag-tag group the press would dub the "Unforgettables," came within a second of upsetting number-one-ranked Duke in a game sportscasters call the greatest ever played. When the players were asked what Pitino's greatest contribution was, many said, "He put the fun back in the game."

Clowning around

The first time I called on Sandy, I was taken aback by her appearance. It's not that she wasn't dressed appropriately. Her gray business suit fit her position as a healthcare executive perfectly. What threw me was the fact that she was sitting behind a large executive desk wearing a red clown nose. As we sat down and began discussing my training programs, I found it difficult to look her directly in the eye. She made no reference to her nose, and conducted the interview as if it weren't there. Unable to contain myself further, I asked her if her hospital treated nose disorders. "That's the worst case of chafing I've ever seen!" I said, laughing.

Sandy laughed as well, removing the fake nose from her own. "We have a pretty tough job to do here," she said. "It's stressful, demanding, and not always filled with much appreciation. We do everything we can to add a little laughter to the daily grind." Sandy went on to reveal that the nose was actually part of my audition. "We don't like to work with people who take themselves too seriously," she said. "I wore the nose to see what your reaction would be." She assured me that I had passed with flying colors.

No laughter zones

For years laughter in the workplace was equated with goofing off. Somewhere along the line we decided that being serious about our work meant being solemn about it as well. A somber tone was equated with productivity (nose to the grindstone), and so we worked hard at being serious. At a time when most companies are faced with the need to get more from less and job stress is a daily fact of life, companies are discovering laughter as the valuable tool it is. Recent research indicates that laughter is a way to:

❖ Reduce stress.

❖ Disarm anger.

❖ Reduce resistance to change.

❖ Stir up creative juices.

❖ Increase morale.

❖ Produce positive attitudes.

❖ Reduce medical and absentee expense.

❖ Increase the acceptance of ideas.

❖ Keep turnover to a minimum.

In short, companies are discovering that laughter and fun are one of the best combinations for employee satisfaction and retention.

Turning failure into victory

1. Accept responsibility for the fun factor in your department. Creating fun is not something you do once or twice a year. It has to be an ongoing part of the environment.

2. Use humor to break stress-generating situations. John Cleese, the comedian and actor, says that a problem that threatens to overwhelm us can often be reduced to its right proportions by the injection of humor.

3. Make work a celebration of individual talents. Find out what talents people have and how they use them outside the workplace and encourage them to share their gift with the team. One manager I know plays the clarinet as poorly as anyone I've heard. But he brings it to work and plays it for every birthday, to the great dismay (and laughter) of his staff.

4. Get more humor in your office. Encourage workers to bring in their favorite cartoons, then route them through the office. Save them and vote for the best one at the end of the week. Save the weekly winners, and vote for the cartoon of the month. Give a humorous prize to the winner. I get my best prizes at the Everything's a Buck store.

5. Model the behavior you want. There's an old saying that we should take our jobs seriously, but not ourselves. It's still good advice. Let your employees see that you support laughter in the workplace and view it as a positive experience for the team.

Mess-Up No. 43

Failure to "prime the pump" (train employees).

"One of the major tasks of the people moving into managerial positions today is going to be helping everyone learn enough, fast enough, to keep up with the business or specialty involved."

—Sharon Kirkman Donegan, President,
Boyle/Kirkman Associates

Years ago the Kingston Trio had a hit record called "Desert Pete." The song told the story of a man wandering in the Little Cactus Desert for three days without food or water. As he was struggling along, he looked off into the distance and saw what he thought might be an old water pump. At first he thought it was a mirage, because the desert heat will play tricks on a thirsty man. But as he drew closer, he realized it was indeed what he thought it was. Desert Pete, parched and dry, ran the last hundred yards and fell at the foot of the pump.

When Pete looked beside the pump, he noticed an old Mason jar full of cool, clear water. He grabbed the jar and started to open it when his eyes fell upon a sign attached to the pump. The sign read "Don't drink the priming water. Use the water in the jar to prime the pump. After getting a prime, refill the jar for the next person." The note went on to read that it would take the whole jar to do the job. Now Pete was in a dilemma. On one hand, he could drink the water and take care of his thirst. If he did, however, none who followed would be able to drink. On the other hand, if he put the water in that old rusty pump and it failed to reach a prime, he would have caused his own demise.

The choice facing Desert Pete is similar to the one facing managers today. Do you take care of your own needs, or invest in those who follow? Managers who take responsibility for the growth and development of their employees do what Desert Pete did. They prime the pump of human potential, and watch that sucker flow! I have an old-fashioned hand pump in my office as a reminder of this critical management obligation.

A simple strategy

Ross Perot, the billionaire businessman and political gadfly, identifies the three most important things managers do as the following: First, take care of the customer; second, earn a profit; and third, teach someone else to do numbers one and two! Perot is right. The need for managers, especially those in smaller businesses, to be effective teachers and trainers has never been greater.

More than ever, success depends on the knowledge of employees and the skill with which they are able to apply it. Companies are more dependent than ever before on their managers to facilitate that growth and development.

The case for training

The benefits to the organization of a consistent, on-going training agenda are considerable. Companies that invest in their staff will find that training:

❖ Helps to manage the effects of change.

❖ Helps to improve productivity and effectiveness.

❖ Helps to develop the skills needed to defeat the competition.

❖ Helps to protect a company's primary asset (its people).

❖ Helps to convey the vision and purpose of the organization.

❖ Helps the organization to create distinction through its people.

❖ Helps to increase job satisfaction and reduce turnover.

Another benefit of training, one often overlooked, is that it is a powerful motivator for the employees who receive it. More than anything, training is a symbol of the employees' value to the company. When a company chooses to invest in its workers, it's saying to those workers that they're important and that they figure in future plans. And that's motivating.

Training is a turn-on

It's not surprising, given the above, that employees want to be trained. They not only want the satisfaction that comes from doing their work well, they want the financial opportunities that go with increased skill and performance. Because training is a symbol of their future with the company, they want the increased self-esteem that comes with this commitment. In addition, they want the increased independence that comes from being more knowledgeable. The bottom line is that employees empowered by training are ready to contribute to the growth of their companies.

Getting it going

Successful training, like all good business practices, begins with a good plan. The plan should identify which individuals should be included in the training, when and how often it should occur, and where it will be conducted. The last issue is what areas that training should cover. Some typical areas of training covered by managers include:

- ❖ Product knowledge and use.
- ❖ Specific training related to the job function.
- ❖ Customer service topics (handling complaints, phone skills, attitude).
- ❖ Communication skills (written, verbal, nonverbal).
- ❖ Technical skills.
- ❖ Personal development issues (time management, problem-solving, education).
- ❖ Team building issues.
- ❖ Conflict resolution issues.

The above list is just a taste of the variety of training topics and opportunities. The key, of course, is to discover which ones are of most value to your staff. The two best ways to find out are to observe your group and pin-point areas of weakness, and to ask employees themselves what they would like. Then just get started.

Turning failure into victory

1. Recognize that training is a powerful symbol. When a manager invests her time (and the company's money) in an employee, the message sent is that the employee figures in the future plans of the organization. Not only does training increase skill, it increases self-esteem.

2. One of the ironies of training is that it can be both motivating and threatening to employees. Assure your group that you're all there to learn and share in an environment of mutual respect.

3. When presenting training, let your group know that their ideas and experiences are an important part of the program. Assure them that they are strongly encouraged to share their thoughts. Tell them questions are also expected and encouraged.

4. Accept the fact that effective training for adults is part knowledge and part entertainment. Spend time developing ways to introduce humor and fun into your training. It's one of the ways adults learn best.

5. Conduct short review sessions of your training within 72 hours of the original program. Studies indicate that when these reviews are conducted, retention of the material increases by nearly 50 percent.

Part 10:
Planning

Mess-Up No. 44

Failure to set challenging and meaningful goals.

"Objectives are not fate; they are direction.
They are not commands, they are commitments.
They do not determine the future; they are means
to mobilize...resources and energies."

—Peter Drucker, *People and Performance*

Everybody has a favorite customer, and as a consultant and trainer, so do I. It's a large construction company just across the river from Louisville. They're a nice bunch of people and they pay their bills on time. But that's not why they're my favorite account. I like these guys because they own a Bell Jet helicopter. And whenever I work with one of their out-of-town offices, I get picked up in their whirlybird and set down in the middle of their parking lot. It's quite a kick, and I always look forward to working with them.

The first time I flew with them, I was so pumped I probably would have worked for free. After a bit, the president got tired of my hints and finally let me have his seat up front beside the pilot. I immediately started playing 20 questions with the fellow. As we flew along no more than 1,000 feet or so off the ground, I asked him if he had to file a flight plan when he took a trip. He advised it wasn't necessary, as long as he never got higher than 1,500 feet in the air. Zipping along at that height, I thought the treetops below us looked pretty close!

Helicopter goals

A flight plan is a report required of pilots by the FAA (Federal Aviation Agency). It details where they're going, when they expect to arrive and when they plan to return from their trip. The exceptions to the rule—as noted above—are helicopters and other aircraft (Ultra Lites) that fly under 1,500 feet. In many respects, these flight plans are like goals. To be effective, they have to be in writing and filed before the trip. I like to refer to unwritten plans as "Helicopter goals." They're acceptable, but only if you don't plan on rising very high.

While many managers agree with the concept of goals in principle, few actually follow through. According to a recent survey, less than 3 percent of all managers have formalized, written goals. Yet without them, they suffer a loss of focus and structure that hampers productivity. Formal goals are not only essential for establishing direction and priority; they are a key component in identifying management values as well.

Setting SUMMIT goals

If you'd like to rise a bit higher, here are six ingredients in my SUMMIT goal setting system that will help bring your flight plans into focus!

Specific. One of the keys to a good flight plan—or goal—is clarity. Is your target clearly defined? Most goals are compromised by the fact that they fail to really define the objective. For example, we want to increase sales "a lot" is not a specific goal!

Useful. Is the goal meaningful to you personally? Any goal that fails to demonstrate personal benefit will have difficulty getting a high level of commitment. There has to be something positive in it for you.

Manageable. If someone offered you a million dollars to climb Mt. Everest, would you do it? I wouldn't. It's not that I'm not motivated by the money; I just know I'm not strong enough to do it. If the effort expended will not yield the expected results, the effort will not be made. A good goal must be "do-able."

Meaningful. Is your goal important to you? In other words, will it bother you if you don't reach it? If the answer is no, then the likelihood of it happening is slim. Only set goals that will make you feel a sense of pride if they are accomplished.

Integrated. Are your goals integrated with each other? Do they fit in with everything else you've planned? Goals to save 35 percent of your income, while buying a new car, and traveling to Europe may not have much synergy.

Tangible. Is your goal recorded in writing? Unwritten goals are only resolutions. And we all know what happens to those.

After you've written a goal, test it in each of the six categories scoring it on a 1 to 5 scale (5 being excellent). Your rating is purely subjective. If your total for all six categories exceeds 25, you have a SUMMIT goal that will take you to the top! If your score is below 25, look at ways to restate your objective to increase effectiveness in the weakest areas.

Fire up that stogie!

As a long time fan of the Boston Celtics, I used to love to watch Red Auerbach at the games. As the coach of the Celtics, Auerbach used to have an intimidating habit. When he felt his team had the game in hand and were on their way to victory (attainment of a goal), he would fire up a rather noticeable cigar. Opponents even developed the habit of looking at Red to see if it were time to toss in the towel! Once, in a very close game, Auerbach lit his cigar with the score tied. In a few short minutes of play, the Celtics blew the game open. I wondered if it was the play of the Celtics, or the psychological intimidation of Red's cigar that caused the change.

Red's cigar was lit in recognition of the accomplishment of a goal. Lighting it before the goal was actually accomplished was a form of visualization for Red. He was seeing the victory in his mind before it was actually accomplished. From Red Auerbach I've learned three rules that lead to a successful and satisfying career. First, nothing happens without goals. The aimless drifting towards objectives normally falls short of achievement. Second, it's important to not just pursue goals, but to believe they will happen. Every day, I mentally picture myself accomplishing the objectives I've set. Lastly, I've learned to take time to celebrate my victories (goals accomplished). I'm leaving the stogie for Red, however.

Turning failure into victory

1. Make a personal commitment to the goal-setting process. Only 2 percent of all Americans have written goals. Yet studies indicate those who set and follow meaningful goals accomplish far more than those who do not. Remember, there's no excellence without commitment.

2. Make sure your business goals are in sync with those of your company. Make sure you have a copy of your company's mission statement and core values so you can see where it intends to allocate resources. Meet with your boss to make sure your goals are compatible with his.

3. Put your goals in writing and share them with someone else to increase personal accountability. Unwritten goals are nothing more than resolutions, and we

all know how quickly those slip out of mind. Make it a point to review your written goals at least once a month to monitor your progress.

4. Don't be afraid to bail out on a bad (unproductive) goal. Sometimes priorities and available resources change. The time devoted to a goal with a poor return on investment may be better spent on one with a higher payback.

5. Model the behavior you expect. If you want goals from your workers, let them see a copy of yours. It certainly helps if others know where you expect to lead the team.

Mess-Up No. 45

Failure to understand the emotions of delegation.

"The winners in the next few decades will be the companies with the most empowered work force."

—Michael Dell, founder and CEO,
Dell Computers

Whenever practical, I like to get to know a company before presenting workshops to their staff. Many times, a part of this getting acquainted process will include a tour around the client's facilities. These tours are not only useful in getting a feel for the culture of a company, they often provide some early indicators of what I might expect later in the workshops themselves. During these tours I observe as much as possible, looking for clues that reveal how the employees of that company feel about their jobs and their company. I pay particularly close attention to what's taped to the sides of filing cabinets or tacked to a wall. I'll never forget the sign I saw pinned up at one company. "Happiness," it read, "is seeing your boss's picture on a milk carton!"

I recall a recent guided tour I took of a facility in the Southwest. The company was in the food service industry. As we walked through the plant, my guide suggested I wander around on my own for a while. "You'll learn a lot more doing your own thing than you will from my spiel," he said. After he left, I continued walking around looking for "culture clues." As I walked past the office of the general manager, I noticed a plaque on the wall with the words "Now Serving" printed in large letters. Under that were two hooks that held cards printed with numbers. "Take a number," the instructions read, "and wait your turn."

About that time I heard a buzzer, announcing a break for the plant crew. I followed several people into the canteen and walked over to the soda machine, where one of the employees was trying to get change for a dollar. "I don't have change," I said to him, "but I'll treat you to a soda." I introduced myself and told the man I would be doing some training programs for their management team. "Good," he said, "they can use it." I asked if I could join him for a few minutes to chat about his perspective on things.

"Off the record?" he asked.

"Sure," I responded.

We talked for several minutes before I mentioned the sign outside the GM's door. I learned that one of the workers had made the sign and given it to him as a joke at Christmas. "Nobody," my guest said, "can make a decision on anything around here. It's not unusual for four or five people to be standing around waiting to ask the guy a question."

"I guess that can be kind of frustrating," I replied.

"Well, to tell you the truth," he said, "it makes the workers feel pretty insignificant. Waiting for information and answers from this guy reminds me of asking my dad for my allowance when I was a little kid."

Later that afternoon, all the managers and I were gathered together for a "get acquainted" session. I was introduced to the general manager, and told him I had noticed his "Now Serving" and "Take a Number" signs by his door. "Isn't that a kick?" he said. "One of the guys on the floor made those and gave them to me for Christmas."

"How did that make you feel?" I asked.

"I know some of the people out there feel bad about having to bother me all the time," he said. "But to tell you the truth, I kind of like it. I find it stimulating when I'm surrounded by a bunch of people asking questions." I asked the man if he thought the people standing in line were equally stimulated. "Why wouldn't they be?" was his reply. "They're interfacing with the boss."

On the surface, you might be inclined to think this manager was a bit of an egotist. In reality, he was a very agreeable man who thought his actions were appropriate. As he told me later, he saw himself as a resource center. "I just want to be available to answer people's questions," he said. What he didn't realize was that his management style had created a cult of dependence. By controlling so much information, it was virtually impossible to get anything done without his direct input. The result was a discouraged and demotivated work force.

The emotions of delegation

Most people would readily agree that managers who fail to delegate are compromising the productivity and efficiency of their departments. At a time when companies need to be flexible and responsive, uninformed and uninvolved workers are a huge liability. Not only does this kind of work culture take away a company's maneuverability, it's one of the greatest factors contributing to the demoralization of staff. Managers unaware of the motivational impact of delegation are creating a staff dependency that could lead to organizational paralysis.

There are few responsibilities a manager carries out that are more emotionally laden than delegation.

Delegate effectively and often and you'll find yourself surrounded by workers who believe in themselves and in their ability to contribute. Fail to delegate and a host of negative emotions emerge. Self-esteem is lowered, job satisfaction is compromised, respect and trust are undermined, and a sense of individual importance is lost. When you consider that the latter is one of the four basic psychological needs of all people, you begin to see how important effective delegation is.

The objective here is not to address the how-to of successful delegation. My purpose is to emphasize the complexity of its emotional impact. Like the employee made to stand in line to talk to his manager, no employee likes to feel like a kid asking a parent for an allowance.

Turning failure into victory

1. Recognize that delegation speaks to the self-esteem and value of each person. When you delegate a worthy task to a subordinate, you are sending a message to that person that you have confidence in his or her talent and ability.

2. Recognize that delegation is a power-sharing activity that reinforces trust. Managers who refuse to share some of the power of their position send dual messages of distrust and insecurity. Managers who share that power create a culture of trust and empowerment.

3. Recognize that delegation addresses the basic need to feel important. Rewarding subordinates with a challenging and meaningful task increases their feelings of significance.

4. Delegate the good stuff. Look at the task you are considering handing off and ask yourself, "Is this something I'd want to do if I worked for me?" If the answer is yes, pass it on!

5. Recognize that delegation is a powerful picture of a person's future. You can tell an employee as often as you like how important he or she is, but you must convey that importance in the form of shared power.

Mess-Up No. 46

Failure to ask the question, "Is this the best use of my time right now?"

"To waste your time is to waste your life, but to master your time is to master your life and make the most of it."

—*Alan Lakein*, How to Get Control
of Your Time and Your Life

Seven hours of grueling interviews had yet to uncover even a possible candidate. The last candidate of the day, a graduate of my alma mater, was my last hope. The interview went well, with the man handling my questions with ease. I finally got to the last one. "We all have areas of weakness," I began, "can you define an area in which you'd like to improve?"

"Well," he replied, "I guess my greatest weakness is plagiarism." Stunned by his response, I said "Plagiarism?"

"Yeah," he continued, "I'm always putting things off till the last minute."

The time trap

Several years ago I was hired by a local college to serve as an adjunct lecturer teaching courses in business management. Hired near the beginning of the term, there wasn't time to select the text, so I went along with what had been used before. When I went to the bookstore to pick up a copy, I was surprised to see a note directing students to purchase a companion book for the course titled *How to Get Control of Your Time and Your Life*, by

Alan Lakein. I picked up a copy of the book, thinking it might be important if the person teaching the class read it first. "Great," I thought to myself. "When am I going to find time to read this?"

The section of the course dealing with time management was not scheduled to be covered until halfway through the course, so Lakein's book got tossed aside. To say the least, that first semester was a hectic one. Not only was I teaching five nights a week, I was working full time trying to build a speaking and consulting business. Adding to that load were my responsibilities to my church, and my activities in my community. I also had a wife and two daughters who thought it might be nice to see me once in a while. The pressure was beginning to take its toll.

One night I got home after everyone else had gone to bed, and went to my office to work on a presentation I had to make to a client the next morning. I fired up my computer and began desktop publishing an elaborate design for the cover of my handout. One of the things I've discovered about desktop publishing is that whatever took you a few minutes before, can now be done in hours. It's not that I'm slow; just that there are so many more options and I find it hard to leave them alone. It was nearly 3 a.m. when I finished and dragged myself off to bed. "I've got to get control of my life," I thought. Then I wondered, "Why does that sound familiar?"

The next morning I discovered why. A quick glance at the syllabus told me that my class that night was supposed to cover the chapter on time management. I looked around on my desk for my copy of Lakein's book, but couldn't find it anywhere. "Have you seen a book on time management lying around," I asked my wife. "I think there's one in the back seat of the car," she replied. Sure enough, it was right there where I had tossed it two months earlier. I pitched it into my briefcase, and headed off for my presentation.

When I arrived at my client's office, I was led to a conference room where a panel had been convened to hear my proposal. I felt confident about the presentation. And why not? My handouts were professional, reflecting the time I had put into them. My PowerPoint presentation matched the handouts, complete with the graphics added the night before. When I left the meeting, I felt pretty confident about getting this company's business. You can imagine my shock later when I received a call telling me the panel had rejected my offer. "Did they give a reason why?" I asked the caller. "To tell you the truth," the man said, "we thought you seemed a bit run-down."

Losing that business was still on my mind that night when I arrived to teach my class. When I opened my briefcase to get my notes out, I saw the copy of Lakein's book lying there. "Geez," I thought, "I forgot to read the book." I'm not sure what happened at that point, but something snapped. "I can't believe it," I thought. "I'm working harder than I've ever worked in my life, and I'm getting nothing accomplished." I looked at my class, and saw a room full of students looking impatiently at their watches. "Ladies and gentlemen," I began, "my name is Mark Eppler, and I'm a time waster."

Time wasters anonymous

It wasn't quite a 12-Step Program, but my confession that night changed the dynamic of the class for the rest of the semester. I was no longer the guru standing in front dishing out pearls of wisdom. I told them I really needed to learn how to get control of my time and life. Because the vast majority of my students were adults attending night class, they had a few time challenges of their own. We agreed that night to read Lakein's book not as "testable material," but for real answers to real problems. We made a pact with each other to not just read, but to apply what we learned. We agreed to hold each other accountable for improvement.

I've included Lakein's book in every class I've taught since. There are many books on the subject, but I like this one best. Although there are a host of tips in the book for getting control of your life, there is one in particular that has made a dramatic difference in how I manage my time. The tip, called Lakein's Question, is to ask yourself several times a day, "Is this the best use of my time right now?" This simple question has caused me to change my activities on countless occasions simply because the answer was "no." Learning to ask this question spontaneously over the years has kept me from pursuing a lot of unproductive tasks.

Time to bail, not invent a better "bailer"

Few time traps are as subtle, or as effective, as activity masquerading as productivity. It's very easy to be deceived into thinking that if you're busy, you must be making something happen. I had an employee several years ago who seemed to be the hardest working person I had ever met. The problem was that nothing of substance ever seemed to get done. His sales finally dropped to the point that I had to take a hard look at his performance.

"What are you working on right now?" I asked one day. "I'm setting up a new data base so we can track account activity," he answered. His desk was covered with manuals and forms. "I'm having a little trouble right now, trying to design what the reports will look like."

"Let me ask you a question," I said. "Is this the best use of your time right now to increase sales?" He started to react defensively. "Hang on," I said, "I'm not saying what you're doing isn't important, but with your sales as low as they are, is this the *best* thing you can do right now to improve them?"

"No," he said, "I guess it isn't."

"Let's find out what is," I said, "and turn this around." This new approach to time management had a very positive effect on the employee's productivity.

Turning failure into victory

1. Ask yourself Lakein's question: "Is this the best use of my time right now?" If the answer is no, choose another task. Then ask the question again. Ask the question often during the day to insure that you are making the best possible use of your time.

2. Recognize that the key is not to be busy, but to be busy on those tasks that can contribute most quickly to your goals and the goals of the organization. The purpose of Lakein's Question is to identify the best task, then do it in the best way.

3. Recognize that the best use of your time may not be the thing you enjoy doing most. Exercise discipline in choosing activities that contribute most to the purpose of your work.

4. Keep Lakein's question in your line of vision until asking it becomes second nature. Put signs around your office, on your computer, on your PDA—wherever you might be making a decision that will result in the allocating of a portion of your time.

5. Advise your staff of your commitment to this time management strategy. Make it clear that while you don't want to be discourteous, you are not going to allow any diversions that take you away from the most important tasks of your day (as defined by Lakein's question).

Mess-Up No. 47

Failure to anticipate the future (plan ahead).

"For who would begin construction of a building without first getting estimates and then checking to see if there is enough money to pay the bills?"

—Luke 14:28 (NLT)

Business consultant Fritz Dressler says predicting the future is easy. It's trying to figure out what's going on now that's so hard! As the saying goes, it's hard to remember that the original objective was to drain the swamp when you're up to your rear in alligators. Despite the many pressures of the present, taking the time to plan for the future is a critical part of the manager's job.

Fail to plan, plan to...

Many managers, it seems, are getting through their careers on the Christopher Columbus Plan. They start out not sure where they are going and end up not knowing where they've been. And they do it all on someone else's money. Despite the critical importance of this key function of management, many managers operate on a day-to-day basis, letting each day's needs dictate their direction. The result is a department operating much like a boat without a rudder. The chances of floating effortlessly into the right harbor are slim or none. A failure to plan results in disorganized and uncoordinated activities that end up costing the organization time, money, and opportunity.

A reflection of company culture

In many respects, the planning process of a company is a reflection of its culture. I've worked with companies where only a handful of people were involved in the planning process. I've worked with companies where planning only addressed financial topics, with little thought given to other competitive issues. The planning process of each of these companies was a direct reflection of their management style and priorities. Both companies suffered from the lack of clear purpose and direction at the lower management level, which was not involved in the planning process.

The best company I've worked with in terms of the planning process involved its entire management team in the process. Companywide planning would begin with a two-day off-site meeting to identify potential obstacles and opportunities to be faced in the coming year. A rough framework of departmental goals consistent with corporate objectives would emerge from these sessions. Each manager then held a similar meeting with the members of his or her department. The initial phase of the planning process ended with each employee being asked to develop personal goals that supported her or his role in meeting company objectives. The process continued throughout the year with regular "check points" to insure that the plan hadn't met with any obstacles, and to identify any changes that may be needed. The continuity of their efforts accounted for a large part of the company's success.

Planning: the process

The first and most important step in the management function is planning for the future and the changes it will bring. Here are a few of the key elements in the preparation of a viable plan:

Plans must be specific. The initial plan of a company must be as specific as possible. Companies that have clear, well-defined objectives tend to have employees who will know what their responsibilities in carrying out the plan will be. The more focused the plan is at the top of an organization, the clearer it is at the bottom. Goals like "good quality" or "great service," while laudable, are not focused enough for effective action. Fuzzy objectives lead to fuzzy outcomes.

Plans must be flexible. A number of years ago I worked with a company that implemented an MBO (Management by Objectives) program that set some aggressive goals for the coming year. Unfortunately, they set their goals and objectives in concrete, and pursued them rigidly. Halfway through the year, their industry suffered an "inventory adjustment" that seriously depressed their business. Rather than make the adjustments needed to their business plan, they proceeded along, closely adhering to their plans. The result was that critical resources were allocated to projects with much lower priorities than those created by the recession.

Plans must be consulted. I was visiting Cape Cod several months ago and was surprised at how many secondary roads there were. It was easy to lose track of where you were and to drift farther and farther from your destination. Without a good map, it's all but impossible to get to your next destination efficiently. By the time we left the Cape, the map we purchased at the Salt Marsh Visitors Center was tattered from all the times we referred to it. A company's business plan should also be frequently consulted to determine if the company is on track or wandering off its chosen path.

Planning should be sequential. The best planning sessions are the ones that follow a logical process. The first step is to set goals (objectives). The second part of the process is to identify the measures that can be taken to reach those goals. After identifying the alternative steps to reaching the goals, those steps must be evaluated against the company's capabilities and available resources. Then the plan should be placed in the hands of those who will be responsible for carrying it out. The last step is to follow up on the progress of the plan to be sure it is being effectively implemented.

Turning failure into victory

1. Ralph Waldo Emerson said, "Make no small plans, they have no magic to stir men's souls." But don't make any unrealistic plans either, because they will be impossible to accomplish!

2. Give planning the time and attention it deserves. Planning is the first and most basic of all management functions, one of the essential responsibilities of today's managers. The manager's plan is his department's road map in unknown territories.

3. Good plans anticipate potential problems and contain "escape clauses." Make sure the plans developed by your company take into consideration obstacles that may arise after the plan is produced.

4. Make your plans and objectives as specific as possible. Remember, fuzzy plans lead to fuzzy performance. And fuzzy performance leads to fuzzy outcomes. However, don't get bogged down in meaningless detail.

5. Make your plans realistic. Goals and objectives that are incompatible with the company's resources will only waste time and money and frustrate workers. Consider all possible options and choose those best linked to the company's capabilities.

Part II:
Company Culture

Mess-Up No. 48

Failure to use symbols of your company's culture.

"Companies that have cultivated their individual identities by shaping values, making heroes, spelling out rites and rituals and acknowledging the cultural network have an edge."

—Terrence Deal and Allen Kennedy,
*Corporate Cultures: The Rites
and Rituals of Corporate Life*

While on a sales trip to Everett, Washington, I had misjudged the time I would need to get to my destination, and found myself nearly an hour early for my appointment. Although the prospect of killing time in a customer's lobby wasn't particularly appealing, it would at least afford me the opportunity to get caught up on my trip notes. As I entered the office and approached the registration counter, my attention was grabbed by a striking display taking up more than half of the spacious lobby. I headed over to check it out.

The display, illuminated behind glass panels, contained the original office used by the founder of the company. His desk was covered with drawings and other paperwork, as well as a coffee cup. A filing drawer left half-open completed the scene. Although the company's founder had died a number of years before, the effect the viewer got was that the man had just stepped out for a minute and would be back at his desk shortly.

Around the display, signs on the glass panels told viewers about how this man had started the company, his early vision for its future, and the principles upon which it was built. These principles are well-known by all the company's employees, because most of the founder's beliefs have been incorporated into quality plans, mission statements and service strategies. Although the founder was gone, he continued to cast a long shadow over his creation. The display in the lobby helps employees connect—symbolically—with the values and beliefs that turned a small company into a global giant.

Symbolic Management

Companies with strong beliefs about what it takes for them to succeed often rely on the stories of past company heroes and heroines to illustrate those beliefs. One such story in particular comes to mind. A company I worked with received a rush order from a customer whose production line was stopped when it ran out of parts. The order absolutely had to ship that day. While the order was being produced, the plant suffered a complete power outage. With the electricity off, the machines used to produce the product could not be run. Because there were no windows in the assembly area, the production group was in total darkness. No way the parts can ship, right? Not according to the rest of the story, which is now a part of that company's symbolic culture.

Without consulting anyone else, one of the assembly operators requested a flashlight from the maintenance crew. Along with another woman, she managed to set up an old arbor press and proceeded to make the parts manually. While one held the flashlight on the assembly tool, the other produced the parts so urgently needed by the customer. The parts were completed on time and shipped as promised. When asked why they took the initiative to get the parts done, one of the ladies replied, "We didn't want to break our promise and disappoint our customer." A picture of these two employees in action hangs in the production area as a reminder to everyone to let nothing get in the way of meeting the customer's needs. Now that's the stuff that cultures are made of.

Culture you can see and feel

Here are a few examples of how a company's beliefs and values can be expressed through symbols:

❖ A sales manager has an old-fashioned hand pump in his office as a reminder to his sales team to "prime the pump" (do the necessary preliminary work) to get things going. The pump has become so much a part of the culture in that office employees often refer to sales calls as "prime" opportunities.

❖ The first ad one company ever ran featured the president dressed up like a clerk in a general store. The ad's message—old-fashioned customer service—is the heart of the company's marketing strategy and a large copy of the photo is prominently displayed at the company's headquarters as a reminder of their core values.

❖ A bell on the wall in a sales department is rung for big orders and other significant accomplishments. The bell has become a symbol of success and a key company belief: work hard and celebrate your victories!

❖ The general manager of a company has two tools mounted on the wall in his office: an ax and a sledge hammer. When people ask about their significance he tells them that both can be used to chop down a tree. One, however, is better for the job! The message: use the right tool for the job.

❖ An aircraft engine company builds a new $40 million learning center, sending a powerful message to employees that their growth and development is important. The center includes a "walk of fame" with pictures of key people over its long history.

Turning failure into victory

1. Look for ways to express your company's values through the effective use of physical symbols. Challenge employees to come up with their own symbols (and the success principles that go with them).

2. Use the company's heroes and heroines (and their stories) to reinforce your company's strongly held beliefs regarding success and what it takes to achieve it. If the founder of your company is a visual part of its success story, make him or her a symbol as well.

3. Don't ignore the symbolism of your company's history. Use pictures to tell the story of the company's beginning, and the people who played a part in it.

4. In the most successful companies, managers take the lead in shaping the culture. Be sensitive to your company's culture and its long-term importance to the organization's success.

5. Recognize that the culture of a company is shaped by its symbols, heroes, and values. Look for ways to present these nonverbally. Visual learning has great impact.

Mess-Up No. 49

Failure to recognize the dangers of cynicism.

"Cynics at work deeply doubt the truth of what their management tells them and believe that their companies, given the chance, will take advantage of them."

—Philip Mirvis and Donald Kanter, *The Cynical Americans: Living and Working in an Age of Discontent and Disillusion*

My seminar on customer service had just concluded when one of the participants approached me and asked if I had a minute to answer a question. "I was just wondering," he asked, "do you really believe this garbage?" The directness of his comment caught me off guard. The seminar had lasted two days and frankly, I was dog tired. I was tempted to shoot him a smug reply ("Gosh no, it's just that your company is too stupid to know better!"). But instead, I opted to redirect. "Before I answer your question," I said, "could you tell me why you asked it?"

"Well," he began, "it's nothing personal, but there's no way your service system will work in this company." I asked why. "For one thing," he said, "there's no buy-in at the top." He continued, casting a wary glance over his shoulder. "We're managed by a bunch of self-serving bureaucrats who would sell a customer out in a second if there were a few bucks in it for them." He went on, picking up momentum. "And another thing, they (management) don't think we can take care of customers, anyway." I asked him if he could give me some examples. "You bet I can," he answered.

The dragon in action

"The other day" he began, "I had a customer call and ask to return a shipment. I figured he was trying to stick it to us, so I told him there would be a 10 percent restock charge. The guy went ballistic. He said he's been buying from us for 20 years, and felt I should waive the charge for a good customer. I'd been through this routine before, so I told the guy I don't have the authority to make a decision on that, but that I would look into it. The guy became very irate and said to just forget it, he'll take his business someplace else." "What's your point?" I asked. "My point is this," he said, "The restock charge was a crummy $25. After 25 years with this company, I couldn't make a $25 decision to save a customer." "I thought you said he was only trying to stick it to you anyway," I commented. "Well, that's true," he responded, "but that's a different story."

The rise of cynicism

For many companies, cynicism has been a fire-breathing dragon waiting for an opportunity to turn business into toast. He's a pretty sneaky character, too. Some "dragons," like the guy I just mentioned, are pretty easy to spot. Other times, the only way you'll know for sure the dragon put in an appearance is to inspect the charred remains of your business. Here are a few indications that cynicism may be creeping into your company:

❖ Sales, fairly consistent in the past, start to sag.

❖ Gross profit margins start to slide due to waste and rework costs.

❖ Customer service, a reflection of employee satisfaction, is uninspired.

❖ Delivery commitments made to customers are routinely missed.

❖ Rejects and returns reach record highs.

❖ The prevailing attitude of many employees is "who cares?"

❖ Distrust and resentment are frequently expressed.

❖ Absenteeism and tardiness rise.
❖ Resistance to change is high since no one trusts management.

The causes of cynicism

I actually thought trust was improving in business until "perp walks" became the story du jour on network television as we entered the 21st century. Every night it seemed some "dirty, rotten CEO" was being led in hand-cuffs to some officious looking car. And these were just the ones who got caught! Some think the salaries of CEOs alone are a criminal act. Consider this: In 1990, the compensation of the top 25 CEOs ranged from $6 to $20 million. Ten years later the range had grown to $30 to $700 million. Makes you feel sympathetic toward all those "poor" pro athletes, doesn't it?

If you're interested in learning more about this important issue, I suggest you read a book called *The Cynical Americans: Living and Working in an Age of Discontent and Disillusion*, by Philip Mirvis and Donald Kanter. Although it's been out for a while, it's the most definitive study to date of cynicism in our country. Reasons for the rise in cynicism include a breakdown in family values, poor examples set by leaders, a lack of heroes and heroines, a judicial system that seems to dispense everything but justice, and a media intent on bombarding us with a barrage of bad news. Not surprisingly, that cynicism has found itself into the workplace.

Slaying the dragon

The objective isn't to fire everyone whom we perceive to be a cynic, but to restore bonds of trust and build productive and satisfied employees. There will be occasions, however, when termination *will* be necessary. When it comes to cynical employees, the worst thing you can do is nothing at all.

Turning failure into victory

1. Keep the lines of communication with employees open at all times, especially if you suspect a dragon is on the prowl. Keep employees informed to build trust and prevent the dissemination of inaccurate information.

2. The primary element contributing to a culture of mistrust is the low credibility of management. If management's credibility is low, reestablishing it must take precedence over everything. Have a frank discussion with employees to determine just where management rates on trust.

3. If you determine your organization to be running rampant with cynics, your goal should be to convert cynics into trusting and productive employees. But recognize that this conversion will occur incrementally.

4. Give employees more control of their jobs to prevent an outbreak of cynicism. Studies indicate that people's sense of control over their jobs has a lot to do with their having supportive attitudes and positive outlooks.

5. Build teams with common purpose. When employees feel like a part of something greater than themselves, their satisfaction in their work rises. Cynicism and skepticism are rarely a problem when employees have the high self-esteem that comes from being a part of a productive group.

Mess-Up No. 50

Failure to tidy up the physical environment.

"Coffee stains on the flip down tray mean (to my customer) that we don't pay attention to engine maintenance either."

—Airline executive (anonymous)

If you travel on the M4 motorway from Dublin to Galway, you'll be greeted along the way with signs saying, "Keep Ireland Tidy." I get a kick out of these postings. The word "tidy" reminds me of a mother's admonition to a child to keep their room clean. The importance of the tidiness campaign, however, is one every working adult in Ireland understands. Impressions are formed quickly, often on minor issues, and as the Irish Development Authority seeks to entice companies to locate in Ireland, they understand the importance of presenting the best possible image.

If you look up the word "tidy" in the dictionary you will see it means "neat and orderly." If there is a message many companies need to receive today, it would be this: "Tidy up your act." Just as tidiness is good for Ireland's image and helps attract business to the country, it is good for companies as they try to attract customers. A messy place of work is hard for customers to tolerate and sends a negative message. When it comes to good business, companies need to learn that neatness and order are highly desirable traits.

One of the benefits of my job is the opportunity to visit all types of companies worldwide. Over the years, I've noticed how often my initial impression of an operation is formed on their "front porch." Several years ago I was conducting a series of off-site seminars for a large metropolitan hospital. During the breaks, the smokers in the group would step outside for a quick puff. Throughout the full-day session, we took four breaks—plus lunch. After the seminar was over, I gathered my belongings and left. As I exited, I was shocked to see more than 100 cigarette butts all over the sidewalk and lawn. I know how many there were because I picked them up.

Neat freak!

Before you get the impression that I'm some sort of compulsive neat freak, let me tell you why I bothered to clean up somebody else's mess. While I was standing by the door, an older couple came up the walk. As they approached, the man looked at the ground and commented, "I guess the pigs got loose again." He asked me if I knew who had made the mess. Feeling like a fool, I fibbed and told him I didn't. I didn't think it would be particularly good for the hospital's reputation for me to give them the credit. Would you want medical treatment from an organization that trashed the environment? I picked up the cigarettes to preserve the image of my client.

Does the physical environment of a business make a difference in how we're perceived? Recently, I was seated on an airplane next to a man who found some dried food on his tray table. "I have a hard time picturing these people servicing the engines of this plane," he complained, "when they don't bother to wipe the trays off." Although I'm not obsessive, I admit that I'm strongly influenced by an organization's appearance. When I get on a plane and find stained and worn fabric, I have to wonder where else they've cut corners.

Carpets can talk

I recently called on an account in New England that would have to rate as my all-time worst in terms of cleanliness. The approach to the office set the stage for what followed. The landscape was overrun with weeds, the grass sorely in need of cutting, the building hungry for a coat of paint. As I reached for the glass door (covered with fingerprints) leading to the lobby, I noticed several yellowing copies of *The Wall Street Journal* behind some shrubs. Inside, things got worse.

Greeting their visitors—directly in front of the receptionist's desk—was one of the largest coffee stains I'd ever seen. Behind the receptionist were a series of pictures, each hanging askew. The walls were scuffed, and in need of painting. The furniture was old, stained, and frayed.

The magazines set out for the visitor were dog-eared and stained by use as coasters. The keys on the public phone in the lobby had brown stains on them. It might be important to mention at this point that this was not a small company. This company, a manufacturer of a high-tech product, employed more than 1,000 people.

I was greeted in the lobby by my contact, who led me down a hall (more carpet stains) to a conference room. Before I could put down my briefcase, my host had to clear away the remnants of the last few meetings held there. "Sorry for the mess," he said as he gathered up some coffee cups and a half-eaten jelly donut. The overflowing ashtray remained. The chairs around the conference room all seemed to be covered with crumbs. The pictures on the wall looked as if they had been hung with the specific objective of matching nothing.

Cleanliness is next to...

Requiring that a workplace be kept clean should be as important as any corporate standard. Companies with high standards will not allow anything less than a neat and well-organized appearance at their place of business. I used to work for a man whom we used to call (behind his back) "Mr. Clean." Cleanliness was so important to this man that he required his managers be involved in cleaning up. Every Friday afternoon, every manager in the company could be seen walking toward the factory with a broom or mop in hand. Always leading the charge was the president of the company.

As a sales manager, I thought my time could be better spent on the phone trying to book business. I wondered if the president had any idea what his "janitorial staff" was costing him. Then one day we booked an order for $350,000 with a communications company in Illinois. Needless to say, we were all very excited. When I called to thank the customer for his business, I asked him what had turned the tide in our favor. "Well," he began, "everybody's prices were pretty close. What made us choose you was the cleanliness of your plant. You could eat off the floors!" There you have it. The order was secured with good old-fashioned elbow grease. My impression of the president went from "neat freak" to "pretty smart guy."

But don't go overboard!

The topic of neatness in the workplace at my seminars always seems to bring out some interesting stories. During a break, one of the participants shared an experience of a boss who was somewhat obsessive about keeping things neat and clean. He issued a memo to all his employees dictating that no candy bars were to be eaten at their desks. "To make sure his rule was being followed," the woman shared, "he used to go through everybody's wastebasket after work looking for candy wrappers." I asked her if anyone had been caught. "No," she replied, "everybody puts their candy wrappers inside a sheet of our expensive company stationary, and crumbles it up. He never checks those."

Turning failure into victory

1. Recognize that the physical state of the workplace is a powerful nonverbal statement of your company's standards. Much like the nonverbal communications of managers, the appearance of your business is speaking volumes.

2. When implementing guidelines about cleanliness, include reasons as well. Advise employees that these standards, if adhered to, will result in everyone taking more pride in their workplace.

3. Recognize that the appearance of your office and plant is a quality statement. People may find it hard to believe that a quality product is produced in a plant where the break area looks like a trash heap.

4. Remember that cleanliness is a pretty good sales tool. When considering two suppliers whose price and products are largely the same, customers may choose the one that presents a better appearance.

5. Recognize that keeping things tidy applies to all aspects of a business, not just to the walls and carpet. Keeping desks and files neat and organized increases productivity by eliminating time lost searching for missing reports and files.

Mess-Up No. 51

Failure to cultivate pride of workmanship.

"If a man is called to be a street sweeper, he should sweep streets even as Michelangelo painted or Beethoven composed."

—Martin Luther King, Jr.

The pride people take in the products they produce or services they render is one of the central elements in the delivery of a quality product. Preserving, as well as enhancing that pride, should be part of the culture of a company, supported and championed by the management team. In this respect, building the esteem of the workers, and reinforcing the value they provide may well be one of the most important functions of a manager. My experience, however, is that this task has been sorely neglected.

Sorry, it's the only one!

Several years ago, I was calling on the purchasing manager of a large manufacturer of aviation products in Canada. We were meeting in the company's main conference room, where I noticed a stunning poster on the wall. It showed the company's product as it appeared in outer space, where it was actually used. Because my company's products had been designed into theirs, I thought it would be exciting for the people in our plant to see the results of their work. Especially in such a stunning setting. I asked the purchasing manager if I could purchase a copy of the print for display in our lobby. "No," she curtly replied.

I thought her response was odd, especially because she offered no further word of explanation. Later, I told one of their engineers what had happened, and asked if I might have offended her by requesting a copy. "No," he responded, "you didn't offend her. That picture is a real sore spot in our company." He went on to explain that when the photograph was first displayed in the conference room, the employees of his company had reacted just as I had. "We all wanted a copy," he said, "but we were told that if everybody had one, it wouldn't be special anymore."

Pride of ownership

When you consider what those employees really wanted—a visual point of release for the pride they felt in their work—the company should have gladly provided the posters. When these employees looked at that poster, they felt a great sense of pride of workmanship. It's the very thing that companies pay top consultants big bucks to help cultivate!

When I ask participants at my seminars to define pride of workmanship, I'm surprised at how shallow the answers often are. Few, it seems, are able to anchor the concept in personal terms. For me, it was a lesson I learned early in life from my grandfather, a man I never knew. The story comes by way of my father who, as a boy, was told by his father to paint some chairs. While my father was working, several of his friends stopped by and asked him to join them in a ball game. My dad quickly finished, then went to ask his father for permission to go. "Did you finish painting the chairs?" my grandfather asked. "Yes, I did," my dad replied. "Well then, let's go inspect them," his dad said.

When they got to the chairs my grandfather looked them overly thoroughly. Before concluding his inspection, he got on his knees so he could look at the seat bottoms. "Robert," he said sternly to my dad, "you failed to paint the bottoms of the chairs." My father replied that no one would look there anyway. "Who's going to know?" he asked. "You will," my grandfather replied, handing a paint brush to my dad.

From this story comes my definition of pride of workmanship. Pride of workmanship doing the extra work not because it will be noticed, but because of high personal standards.

Creating a culture of pride

Pride in performance occurs when men and women of character are willing to stamp their names on the product or service they create—in spirit, if not in fact. These people are willing to do so when they're allowed to impact on the creation of the product, when their proposals and ideas are valued and heeded. To solve the problem, get people involved. Give them credit for their achievements (see Mess-Up No. 1). Reward them for their diligence. Create a culture of pride. The truth is, you can't afford not to. The cost of reworking bad products is just too high.

Turning failure into victory

1. Encourage people to take pride of ownership in the work they do. Many companies ask their employees to sign the products they create in an attempt to link them to their work. Whether they sign or not, their "signature" (good or bad) is all over their work.

2. There's a saying that goes, "If you haven't got time to do it right the first time, when will you find time to do it over?" Making a commitment to do work right the first time is evidence of personal pride.

3. Honor the worker, not the job. The station that a person occupies in life says nothing about his or her personal worth. When workers feel their work is appreciated and acknowledged, they will go the extra mile to meet those expectations.

4. Acknowledge excellence. Whenever people exceed the expectations of the customer in their work, take time to praise and reinforce that effort. Don't let a good behavior expire for lack of recognition.

5. Create a hall of fame. Acknowledge those employees who have consistently demonstrated a commitment to high quality work. Induct them into the hall, and make them heroes in a culture that honors excellence.

Mess-Up No. 52

Failure to understand that when graciousness declines, the end is near.

"Every action done in company ought to be with some sign of respect to those who are present."

—George Washington

The first time I ever made sales calls with Don, I knew he was an unusual person. He's one of those rare individuals who have the ability to make the people he meets feel important—genuinely so. Don's style is a unique combination of courteous consideration, along with a disposition to oblige the requests of others. Some people, meeting Don for the first time, might think his treatment almost deferential. Because deference is usually associated with the need to acquire something, it doesn't apply to Don. He's one of those fortunate people who, because of the success of a previous business, get to do what he wants to do. Don's style is the one he chooses, not the one he feels is necessary for booking an order.

George had it right

Our society has certainly moved away from the civility George Washington thought so important for success in life. Washington, at the age of 14, thought good behavior so essential that he drafted a list of personal guidelines he called *122 Rules for Civility and Decent Behavior in Company and Conversation.* Here are a few of Washington's pointers:

1. Speak not evil of the absent, for it is unjust.

2. Speak not injurious words, neither lie in jest or earnest; scoff at none although they give occasion.

3. Break not a jest where none take pleasure in mirth; deride no man's misfortune, though there seems to be some cause.

4. Associate yourself with men of good quality if you esteem your own reputation; for it is better to be alone than in bad company.

5. Use no reproachful language against any one; neither curse nor revile.

Goodwill demonstrated by managers facilitates everything from creativity to teamwork. Contrast Washington's rules of behavior with today's standards, however, and you can see that we've strayed off the path of decency and respect.

When graciousness declines

In business today, graciousness takes a back seat to arrogance. Sometimes that arrogance is tangible, as in the case of a major league baseball player who expressed his displeasure with an umpire by spitting in his face. More frequently, that arrogance is expressed toward employees by managers who esteem themselves greater than their peers. Graciousness is fast becoming an outmoded concept in business. While many may think this an obsolete concept in today's kill-or-be-killed competitive environment, studies indicate a lack of civility can seriously hurt a company's performance. Peter Drucker, one of the world's most respected authorities on business management, notes that "when graciousness declines, the end is near."

Graciousness—courtesy and kindly consideration—can take an average company and turn it into a solid performer. Companies that put an emphasis in these areas can expect benefits such as:

- ❖ Employees who feel valued and appreciated.
- ❖ Reduced friction and conflict.
- ❖ Higher employee self-esteem (and greater productivity).
- ❖ Team spirit, a greater sense of being a part of the whole.
- ❖ Greater customer loyalty.

Get the soap

Those people who have worked for me over the years know I have strong feelings, as did George Washington, against the use of profanity in the office. When I hire a new person, I always take a few moments to share some of my strongly held beliefs about how I expect people to relate to each other. At the top of my list is the language one uses. Nothing reduces your standards of excellence as much as vulgar words. They devalue your ideas and concepts, and may even prevent their adoption by others.

More than anything, profanity is a positioning statement. First, it shows that your command of the language is poor. People resort to cussing when their ability to express themselves is limited by their vocabulary. Second, it projects a lack of professionalism. Third, it projects an attitude of indifference toward customers. Companies that allow their employees to use profanity in the presence of their customers are saying, "I'm willing to risk offending you." No one ever lost an order because they refrained from using bad language

Turning failure into victory

1. Recognize that graciousness is a standard of excellence that is not incompatible with the need to be assertive, aggressive, or competitive. Proper behavior can only serve to strengthen your position. In fact, in a world where so many companies and products are alike, good manners and graciousness can actually be a competitive advantage.

2. Make sure your staff understands the basics of business etiquette. Many companies, recognizing this as a competitive advantage, are sending their employees—especially those with contact with the public—to seminars to reinforce this needed skill.

3. Make sure your position regarding proper conduct in your office is understood by everyone. If someone's behavior is not acceptable, do not hesitate to draw it to that person's attention.

4. Accept the responsibility for taking the lead in your department when it comes to etiquette and graciousness. Like it or not, the actions of managers become the accepted standard.

5. Model the behavior you expect. Treating people in the manner in which you wish to be treated hasn't been improved on much over the years as far as advice goes.

Part 12:
The Basics

Mess-Up No. 53

Failure to understand that the real winning edge comes from creating value, not products.

"There's no such thing as a commodity product. All things being equal, you must learn to sell your distinction of doing business."

—Theodore Levitt,
The Marketing Imagination

I remember the day well. It was one of those glorious spring mornings where the winter chill is sent scurrying by warmth that drives everyone out of doors. I had a couple of errands to run, and this was a perfect day for the task. My first stop was the local hardware store. While I was checking out I commented to Bill, the proprietor, that owning a hardware store seemed like a great way to make a living. Bill looked at me and commented, "Mark, you're in here all the time. I bet you'd make a great hardware man yourself." One thing led to another, and before long, I was in the hardware business.

The grand opening

I was in the hardware business long enough to realize that it was aptly named. It was hard, and it was wearing. And extremely competitive. I remember the day of my store's grand opening. I had asked suppliers to donate gifts to be given to the first customers, and I had received a generous response. The best prize was a solid brass door latch set valued at nearly $200. The prizes were arranged on a table, so each customer could make a selection. The first customer would obviously have the best choice.

When we opened our doors that morning, the first customer was a local retiree named Homer with a reputation for squeezing a penny. When he walked through the door, we gave him a big greeting and officially proclaimed him First Customer. After we took a couple of pictures, I led Homer over to the gift table and informed him that he could make the selection of his choice. It didn't take Homer two seconds to grab that solid brass door latch set. After he had made his selection, I asked him what Eppler's S & T Trustworthy Hardware could do for him. "I really don't need anything," he drawled. Surprised, I asked why he had come by. "Well," he said, "I was at your competitor's store yesterday and his screws were two for a dime. Yours are 6 cents a piece. I just came by to tell you your price is a little high." With that, Homer turned and left, his prize tucked neatly under his arm.

The harsh reality of the hardware business is that the products sold are largely commodity products. In other words, features and benefits are the same. It's like being a banana salesman. What can you say about your banana that I can't say about mine...it's got a zipper? The competitive pressures were only increased when a large discount store opened up nearby. It was a continual source of frustration that products offered at retail by the "big guys" were often sold at prices lower than what we paid our wholesalers. For my business to survive, I had to find a way to lower my prices.

The deal of the century

One day, my sales rep came by with an offer he said I couldn't refuse. It seemed that one of his customers had ordered a display rack of leather gloves, but couldn't afford to take them. Rather than have them shipped back, the supplier told my rep to get whatever price he could for them. I was able to purchase the gloves, which normally retailed for about $20 a pair, for the bargain price of just $2 a pair. "Here's my opportunity to give the discount store a run for its money," I thought. I priced the gloves at $5 a pair, and waited for them to jump out the door.

The gloves, prominently displayed beside the cash register, did not jump out the door. As a matter of fact, they settled in for a long winter's nap instead. Over the period of a year, I sold only one pair of the gloves. I was complaining to my sales rep one day that his deal of the century had turned out to be something less. He looked at my display and said, "You've got them priced too low." I asked him what he was talking about. "Raise the price and they'll go." After he left, I priced each of the gloves at $14.95 a pair. I then put up a sign advertising them as a sale item at $9.99. Within a month, I sold 30 pairs of leather gloves.

When it comes to learning about the basics of business, I acquired more knowledge from my four years in the hardware business than I did in graduate school. I learned a lot about why people buy, and why they do not (more of the latter). I learned that value was in the eyes of the beholder, and that price often had little or nothing to do with conveying worth. One of the greatest lessons I learned, however, was that the real winners in the hardware business—in any business—learn to augment the products they sell. To enhance the "basic good" with something else, something that takes the product out of the generic category.

Understanding value

By definition, value is the buyer's perception of the ability of your product or service to satisfy his or her need. The key word in that definition is perception. If the perceptions of value are fulfilled, the customer is satisfied. If they are not, the customer is unhappy. How unhappy will be determined by the gap between what is received and what was expected. Customers don't buy products; they buy satisfaction of a want. How much it satisfies is the value rendered.

Although I thought at the time that the hardware business was the most competitive industry I had ever seen, I've since learned that the same level of competitive pressure is felt in nearly every business. Winners in today's hyper-competitive business market understand the need to create and sell value, not just a product.

Why are these value issues so important to management? Because a very large portion of the value added to products is provided by the employees of a company. Here's a good example. My wife recently went to a building supply center to buy me a jigsaw for my birthday. Knowing nothing about jigsaws, she asked the sales clerk for advice. He asked her a few questions to determine which would be the best model for her purposes. After listening carefully to her responses, he recommended a model one level below the professional model, but well above the hobby level. He even offered to check the stock area for one that may have been left over from a recent promotion that included a free carrying case. Although my wife may have been able to find the saw cheaper elsewhere, the extra value provided by the employee's superior service more than offset that concern.

Turning failure into victory

1. Take the time to talk to your staff about what you really sell. Make sure they understand the difference between a generic product (all things equal) and an augmented product (one enhanced by those who create it and sell it).

2. Use exemplary customer service to create the distinction necessary to add value to your product. Remember: "All things being equal, sell your distinction of doing business."

3. Correctly define your business in terms of outcomes: the end result of the customer having purchased your product. Teach your employees that the real product is what the customer experiences when the product is put to use.

4. Teach employees the concept of value. When employees understand the concept of value, the manager is able to shift his focus from the tangible (the product, service, paycheck, and so on) to the intangible (needs, satisfaction).

5. To succeed in business, companies must be constantly adding to the value of the customer's experience. The only way to know what he considers valuable is to ask the customer himself what it is.

Mess-Up No. 54

Failure to understand that nothing happens until everybody sells something.

Dedicated to Al Newman (1948-2003), a great salesman.

When I accepted a position working for a small electronics company several years ago, I learned quickly that you often have to wear many hats in a company of that size. Although hired to be the head of sales and marketing, my responsibilities included a number of non-sales tasks, including sweeping up the shop on Friday evenings (the "and all other duties as assigned" portion of my job description). Cross-functional communication in this company was great, because there were no distinct divisions between departments and responsibilities—everybody would have to pitch in with tasks other than those he or she was officially assigned to.

Part of the philosophy of this company was that all employees should consider themselves salespeople. "Nothing happens until somebody sells something," the owner liked to say, "and *everybody* sells something!" The message was clear. If you wanted to work for his company, you had better learn to peddle. The message wasn't figurative. The owner wanted every employee, whether talking to customers or selling the image of the company to the community, to be capable of selling.

Being the sales expert at the company, I was often accompanied on my customer calls by managers from other departments to provide them with some field experience. This wasn't a passive learning experience on the part of these people. They were expected to be able to tell the customer how their department was focused on meeting customer needs. On one trip, Al Newman, our vice president of finance came along to get some field exposure.

Making it happen

We started our trip in Northern California where we made a dozen or so calls on engineers and buyers in Silicon Valley. Because my presentation varied little, my partner had ample opportunity to see how the products were presented to the customer. After three days in San Jose, we caught a flight to Los Angeles, where I was scheduled to conduct a training program for a new distributor.

Unfortunately, the night before going to Los Angeles, I elected to try sushi for the first time. I wasn't all that enamored with the stuff, but my sales rep kept telling me how "totally awesome" it was, so I ate it. The next morning during my presentation, I began to feel something less than totally awesome. About 10 minutes into the program, I tossed the microphone to Al and made a quick exit. He was now responsible for making the presentation.

When we returned home, I was surprised when the president of our company came back to my office to congratulate me on a great job in Los Angeles. "Boy, you must have been super," he said. It turned out that the president of the distributorship had called the president of our company to compliment him on the fantastic job his guy did. Because he had not identified who the "guy" was, our president assumed it was me. I let him know that Al had won the day with an outstanding training session built on what he knew about our company culture (an important part of our sales program), and what he had learned in the 12 sales calls he had accompanied me on over the three days preceding the training session.

When I thought about it later, it occurred to me that our president was right. Nothing happens until somebody sells something and everybody sells something. In business today, every member of the organization must be prepared to "make the case" for the company. An organization's sales quotient is literally the sum total of its people. A good example of this is demonstrated in the effort one particular company with which I was associated made to secure a customer's business.

Team-selling

The order we were trying to secure was an important opportunity for our company. After making a sales presentation to the prospect at their facility, we were informed that the next step in the purchase process would be an on-site audit of our facility by their commodity buying team. When they arrived for the inspection, the first order of business was a meeting with all department managers. During the session, all of our managers were asked questions about their specific duties. Many of the answers required not only technical expertise, but a little salesmanship as well. After the meeting, our visitors split up with the managers of the other departments for longer one-on-one sessions. Later, when we received notification that our company had been selected to receive their order, we were told that one of the primary factors in deciding in our favor was the selling skill of our engineering, purchasing, and quality control people. "Everybody at your company sells," we were told. "It's like your whole company is one big sales team!" Because there were a number of other companies that matched our price and qualifications, this extra dimension of companywide salesmanship was what made the difference and secured the order for us.

Who's selling who?

It was undoubtedly the strangest sales call I had ever made. My company was designing products for use by a manufacturing operation in Toronto. The company had expressed concerns about doing business with an unknown supplier, so we had arranged to visit their plant and make an introductory presentation. As we walked in the front door, we were surprised to be greeted by a sign welcoming each of us by name. Most companies don't bother extending such greetings to salespeople.

While we were signing in at the registration desk, we were greeted by a salesperson. In many companies, this person would be considered the receptionist. The sign over her desk, however, said "Sales Department." The woman behind the desk was very courteous as she inquired about the purpose of our visit. I told her who we were there to see, and she made the appropriate call. As we were waiting for our appointment, the receptionist asked us if we were familiar with her company. I told her it was our first visit, so she brought us several brochures that provided information on her firm. "We're very proud of what we do," she smiled, "and we do it very well."

When my contact came to the lobby to meet us, he was wearing a badge that displayed his name and the words "Sales Department." Because I knew he worked in engineering, I asked him about the badge. "Oh," he laughed, "everyone in our company works in sales." As he led me through the office, I noticed the many signs hanging from the ceiling. One read, "Sales Department— Purchasing Done Here!" Another, "Sales Department— Accounting Done Here!" Every department in the company, it seemed, was a sales department.

When we arrived in his area, our host asked us if we knew anything about his company. We told him we didn't, but were looking forward to learning more on our visit. "Well," he said, "the first thing we need to do is tour the plant so you can see the product being made." Instead of leading us back to the plant, however, he took us to the front of the building and led us into the corporate board-room. There he proceeded to give us an enthusiastic multimedia presentation on what his company made and how it worked. The plant tour followed.

As we completed our tour and headed back to the engineering lab, I commented to our guide that I thought he had missed his calling. "Instead of engineering," I said, "you ought to be in sales." "I am," he grinned. I remembered the signs. "Well, what do you hope to sell me?" I asked. "Stock," he said laughing. Although the engineer was joking, it occurred to me that if this company were to go public, I would be interested in buying their stock, thanks in no small part to the selling efforts of my "tour guide." Companies that succeed in training and encouraging all of their employees to champion the cause of the company will have a significant advantage over those leaving that task to the people in the sales department.

Turning failure into victory

1. Recognize that selling opportunities are everywhere, and encourage your staff to make the most of them. In addition to selling products, employees should sell the company to the community from which it will need to a draw a steady flow of candidates for other positions.

2. Selling is often more a matter of passion and enthusiasm than it is a technical skill. All employees, by speaking enthusiastically about their employers, can be excellent sales representatives. Part of the reason our VP of accounting did so well was the pride he conveyed in the company's products. This is a sales approach that no amount of training can provide.

3. Remember, what customers want most is someone who will listen to their requests and respond to their needs. One of the most persuasive things we can do is listen (see Mess-Up No. 4). Listen intently (including to what remains unsaid) to sell successfully.

4. Selling skills are important regardless of job title or responsibilities. Everyone needs to sell—whether it's their ideas, needs, or vision. Understanding basic salesmanship is beneficial in any business situation.

5. Accept responsibility for the fact that, in the team-sales approach of the 21st century, everyone in the organization is responsible for the promise to the client. Selling, then making good on the promises rendered, is everyone's job, from those in production to those in the corporate suites.

Mess-Up No. 55

Failure to grow the business.

"When employees understand the economics of business, they feel, think, and act like owners."

—Jim Schreiber, Herman Miller executive

Adolph Rupp, the legendary coach at the University of Kentucky, was certainly one of the more intimidating, if not colorful, figures in sports. The winningest coach in basketball, Rupp was known for his off-the-cuff quips, usually laced with sarcasm and profanity. He minced few words in letting others know what he thought, or where they stood. After one hard-fought loss, a reporter asked Rupp if he thought playing well wasn't as important as winning. "If winning isn't important," Rupp growled, "What the hell are the score boards for?" Winning is important, especially in business where livelihoods depend on it. That's why it's essential that every employee "know the score."

A dip in the (bonus) pool

Rupp's comment reminded me of a company I consulted several years ago that decided to share a percentage of its annual profits with its employees. Although the shares were modest, the staff appreciated having a piece of the action. While the company was good about sharing the wealth, it was not so good in sharing the information related to how that wealth was generated. The only thing the employees knew was that if there was anything left over at the end of the year, it went into the "bonus pool." As long as they were allowed to take a dip in that pool, the employees seemed content to let management mind the store.

After four years of continuous growth, the company experienced what employees believed to be their best year ever. Sales increased by 25 percent, shipments by 15 percent. Overtime work had touched everyone as the company struggled to meet increased demand with the same staff. As one worker commented to me later, "We didn't mind the extra work; we figured there would be fewer slices of a larger pie." As the end of the year approached, everyone assumed this would be the year bonuses really amounted to something.

Although this company had achieved record sales and shipments, it had set a few other records in the process. Maintenance, long overdue on key pieces of machinery, had been completed during the year. This was a major expense. Several new pieces of tooling, needed to keep raw materials flowing, were purchased. The obsolete inventory write-off was a record high as well. Purchase discounts, previously received, were forfeited as the company chose to reduce its inventory expense. A new advertising program had increased that expenditure tenfold over what it had been in prior years. None of these expenses was shared in advance with employees.

Santa with an empty bag

The company's practice in the past had been to hand out the checks during the annual Christmas party (the president liked playing Santa Claus). The mood at the party that year was one of enthusiasm, excitement, and great expectation—until Santa got up to speak. The look on his face and the tone of his voice spoke volumes. "I'm afraid I've got some bad news," he began uncertainly. After stumbling through some abstract explanations about inventory, carry-forwards, and write-offs, he finally got to the bottom line. "The fact is," he summarized, "we just didn't make any money." Faced with a stony silence, he continued speaking awkwardly about the "cost of doing business." He finally just sat down.

The impact of Santa's "empty bag" was not a positive one. Employees at the party broke up into smaller groups for mini-gripe sessions. "How the heck" one employee demanded, "can we ship so much and not make any money?" Another wanted to know how the company could give out bonuses for 5 percent growth the year before, but have nothing for five times as much growth this year. "If you ask me," a disgruntled worker muttered, "I think the guys driving the Cadillacs are pocketing it all this year." "No way we didn't make money," an office worker added as she picked up her coat to leave.

When this story was related to me by the president of the company, I asked him what he thought his greatest mistake had been. "Starting this stupid profit sharing plan," he replied, half-joking. "Actually," he continued, "our greatest mistake was overlooking the fact that the majority of our staff—including a lot of managers—just didn't understand how a company makes money."

Of all the mistakes a manager can make, letting his or her staff be uninformed about profits may be the greatest. Unless the employees understand how their actions affect the company's ability to make money, how can they make decisions that support that company's objectives? It would be like playing basketball without keeping score.

Turning failure into victory

1. Tell everyone in advance of the company's commitment to share financial information with its employees. If certain information—such as salaries—cannot be shared, explain why that is necessary. Make this explanation credible, because it's your first step to building trust and credibility.

2. Provide training to help employees understand the company's financial information. Create a positive environment for this training by letting people know in advance when it will occur, and what the objectives will be. And always assume that everyone is starting from scratch. Remember, this information will be intimidating to many.

3. When sharing information, make it a professional presentation with visuals and handouts. One company I know actually cuts up a dollar bill at it notes what percentage goes where. The little piece left is a good visual, too.

4. Before getting into things like income statements and balance sheets, start with the most important item: profits. This is the lifeblood of the organization, and there

isn't an employee in the company who can't do something, whether directly or indirectly, to effect profits.

5. Once your group understands the financial figures, make sure they get them on a regular basis. Remember, the time to tell people they will not be getting a bonus check is not at bonus time.

Mess-Up No. 56

Failure to rise to the occasion.

"The dogmas of the quiet past are inadequate to the stormy present. The occasion is piled high with difficulty, and we must rise to the occasion."

—Abraham Lincoln

Most people, in looking back over their lives, can identify some seminal moment when their view of life began to come into focus. For me it occurred just short of my 15th birthday, when I entered an Optimist Club Speech Contest. The contest began at the local level, where I was assigned a club member to act as my coach. As luck would have it, I was given a rather dour man who also happened to be the town dentist. It was difficult for him to find time to work with me, so I had to come to his office and give my speech while he worked on his patients. I remember one time reciting my speech, and feeling like I had really nailed it. I looked to my coach for praise and heard, "Spit."

I told my parents about my frustration with my coach. They talked it over, and decided that they would help me prepare. My father, a Presbyterian minister and no stranger to the art of persuasive speaking, helped me craft the speech and perfect its delivery. Just outside our home, there was a grove of persimmon trees where Dad and I practiced every evening when he got home. He used to hold a rolled-up newspaper in his hands, and every time

I mispronounced a word or put emphasis in the wrong place, I would feel a gentle tap on the head from the paper. It was my clue to start over. On more than one occasion, with the sun setting and errant persimmons stuck to the bottoms of my shoes, I would beg Dad to quit. His response was always the same. "You can have whatever you want," he'd say, "if you're willing to do the necessary work." And then we'd start again.

After I finished with Dad in the persimmon grove, I would begin work inside with my mother who had distinguished herself in college as a writer and amateur actress. Our practice sessions, held in the living room, which afforded a little privacy from taunting siblings, always began the same way. Mom had a little box that contained 10 bobby pins. Every time the speech was presented correctly, I received both praise and a bobby pin. Every time I made a mistake, I was encouraged, but also forced to surrender a pin. The practice would end whenever I succeeded in getting all 10 pins. On no occasion was I allowed to quit until I had succeeded in swiping all the pins.

And the winner is...

To this day I can remember giving that speech. I remember my excitement when I walked into the little hometown club and discovered how much effort they had put into making that night a special one. A stage had been built by one of the high school teachers, with black drapes behind it for dramatic effect. A spotlight and microphone helped to turn a room in the community center into Carnegie Hall in the minds of the contestants. That night I gave the speech of my life and walked away with the grandest trophy I had ever seen. Afterward, pictures were taken of me, the club president and the dentist, who received credit for being my coach.

After winning at the local level, I competed—and won—at the regional contest. This enabled me to advance to the state finals to be held in Lexington. Because the finals were several months away, I asked my parents if we could take a break. They agreed. Several times over the next few weeks, I received gentle reminders that it might be wise to begin preparing again. Their approach, however, had become less demanding. They were no longer insisting on practice. Having taught me some valuable lessons at the beginning, they were now allowing me to learn some painful ones on my own.

On the day of the contest, I knew I was in trouble. As Dad and I drove east on Interstate 64 to Lexington, he asked if I wanted to run over my speech a few times in the car. I had practiced the speech early that morning in front of my mirror, and was shocked at how much I had forgotten. I remember still the hot flashes I felt as I struggled to recall the lines of my speech. I told Dad I didn't think reciting in the car was necessary. I said I felt pretty comfortable with my chances. The truth was, I didn't want to risk the possibility that he'd turn the car around and go home when he heard me recite!

That day in Lexington was the longest of my life. There were 12 contestants from all over the state, and each deserved to be there. I presented third and, to my credit, delivered the speech without forgetting a single word. What I did forget, unfortunately, were most of the little details that had made my presentation so effective before. I was so focused on the words, that I lost the impact of the ideas. The close, which my father taught me to deliver with passion and conviction, was raced through so I could sit down. When I finished, one of the other contestants whispered, "I'm sure you'll win." I knew she was lying. The top three finishers were given trophies. I rode home that evening empty-handed.

Deserve the victory you seek

Losing that day in Lexington bothered me for years, but it wasn't until two decades later that the reason came to me. I happened to be in London in 1986 when Winston Churchill's wartime headquarters was first opened to the public as a museum. A longtime Churchill fan, I was excited as I descended the steps leading to the underground command post. Below, the various rooms were laid out as they were when last in use: the war room with its maps and ship locations; the secret communications room where Churchill spoke with Roosevelt; the tiny cubicles where the staff slept; the slightly larger bedroom of Prime Minister Churchill. The museum was a visual masterpiece.

As we were moving through the exhibit, our guide asked us to pause and listen to the words of "the great man himself." As we stood there in the dim lighting of the war room, Churchill's voice began to roll over us. His words were filled with alarm and hope. He exhorted the British people to never give up, to fight to the end. Then, in words I'll never forget, Churchill said, "We cannot guarantee that we will win. We can only guarantee that we will deserve victory." What had bothered me for so long since that contest was not the fact that I had lost. What bothered me, I finally realized, was that I didn't deserve to win. I had failed to *rise to the occasion.*

"I'm sorry, you didn't get the order"

The words from the buyer on the other end of the phone hit like a George Foreman uppercut. After four months of extraordinary effort on the part of my department, a sale that would have had a dramatic impact on our fortunes had been given to another company. The buyer thanked us for our trouble and said, "To tell you the truth, you guys deserved the business. Unfortunately, the rest of the selection team opted for a larger, better-known firm."

Some would feel that was not much in the way of consolation, but to me it had great impact. In that one little phrase, the buyer succeeded in taking the sting—not the disappointment—out of the loss. Instead of dreading to share the news with my group, I was actually looking forward to it. The next morning, I gathered my department in the large conference room. When they walked in, they were greeted by a wide array of pastries, bagels, fruit, juices, coffee, and other surprises. I started the meeting by welcoming them to what I called a "Breakfast for Champions." "Did we get the order?" one of our service coordinators asked excitedly. "No, we did not." I replied. "They chose another supplier."

The noise in the room dropped dramatically. "Well, what are we celebrating?" someone asked sarcastically. "We're celebrating the fact that, in the buyer's eyes, we deserved to get the business," I said. I went on to tell them how proud I was of their efforts, and that I believed there was nothing more we could have done. "I would rather lose deserving to win," I said, "than win deserving to lose." An hour later, the employees went back to work with heads held high, feeling like the winners their efforts proved them to be.

Turning failure into victory

1. Teach your employees the value of deserving to win. Tell them that praise and reward will be based on their effort, and not just the outcome.
2. Teach your group that, despite successes in the past, future victories will not be reached with "cruise control" engaged. Emphasize the need for a strong effort every day.
3. Sweat the little stuff. Victories are seldom won in one fell swoop. They are the sum total of many smaller efforts. Teach your staff that details count, and to take care to mind them.
4. Teach your employees the elements of success. Teach them the values of victory, as well as its glories.
5. Celebrate your staff's deserved losses as much as its hard-earned victories. The only losses a manager should hold as unacceptable are those that are deserved.

Part 13:
The Big One

Mess-Up No. 57

Failure to practice in reality what
you learn in theory.

"A winner is someone who recognizes his God-given talents, works his tail off to develop them into skills, and uses these skills to accomplish his goals."

—Larry Bird, professional
basketball player

There's a lot of pressure when you write a book with 57 chapters to make the last one the best one. In the movie *Amadeus*, Salieri said that you've got to end with a bang so people will know you're through. Hopefully, that's what I'm about to do. The story I share with you is as it occurred. Life has a way of yielding its most profound lessons in the simplest of ways, and if we're not looking for them, it's often easy to miss them entirely. This story certainly bears that out.

The door-to-door salesman

When I started my business several years ago, I leased office space in one of those all-in-one facilities where a receptionist, fax machine, and copier were shared by the occupants. The building was U-shaped, with single-room offices off both sides of the hallway. The problem was that people, often thinking individual offices had their own waiting areas, would come in without knocking. To keep surprises to a minimum, most of us kept the doors open. One day I was making an important telephone call, however, and had closed the door for a little privacy. Suddenly, my door burst open and a very large man lunged inside. If you've ever seen Kramer make an entrance on the popular TV show *Seinfeld*, you know exactly what I'm talking about! The man covered the distance to my desk in one long stride and began unfolding what I first thought was a large road map. I realized, as the man struggled to open it, that it was one of those "unbeatable deals" where you could buy 50 pots and pans for the low, low price of $19.95. The man looked at me uncertainly and asked, "Would you like to buy some pots and pans?" I was sitting there with the phone to my ear, which I thought was a pretty good indication that I was already occupied. "Look," I replied, "I'm on an important call."

The man looked a little embarrassed, and quickly refolded his paper. I assumed he was leaving, and was a little surprised—not to mention annoyed—that he only went as far as the doorway where he took up watch like a sentinel. Seeing that the man was not going to leave, I asked the person I was speaking with if I could call him back. When I hung up, I said to the man in my grumpiest voice, "Is there something I can do for you?!"

The man crossed the room and began opening his brochure again. "Would you like to buy some pots and pans?" he repeated. I looked him sternly in the face and said, "No, I would not." "That's okay," he said shoving the map aside, "how about children's books?" I informed him that I had no small children at home. "No problem," he said diving into his bag again. He extracted a blue box with a red cross on the front of it. "How about a first aid kit?" he said, breathlessly. I looked him squarely in the face and said, "I don't want to buy anything."

The man looked a little dejected as he gathered his wares and headed toward the door. Pausing at my door, he noticed the name of my company. "What do you guys do," he asked? Annoyed at the amount of my time that was being wasted, I replied sarcastically, "Well, among other things, I teach people how to sell things." As soon as I said it I realized it was a big mistake. The man turned, came back across the room and asked, "What did I do wrong?"

Generally speaking, I'm not inclined to give free advice to people who wander in off the street. But there was something in this man's voice that touched me, a real note of sincerity. I glanced at my watch, then said, "Sit down for a minute and we'll talk about it." I wanted to find out what the man knew about selling, so I asked a question. "Which is more important in selling a product, features or benefits?" He looked at me for a second then said, "I'm not sure I understand." "Well," I continued, "imagine that you're buying a sports car and the salesman says that it will go from 0 to 60 in 2.3 seconds. Is that a feature or a benefit?" The man responded enthusiastically, "That's a benefit!" "Not if you never have a need to go that fast. It's only a benefit if you need it," I replied.

I explained my theory that it was easier to meet a need than it was to create one. "I think I understand where you're headed," he said, "but could you do me a favor?" I asked what it was. "Show me how you'd sell this first aid kit," he said. I picked up the kit and told him to pretend to be an office worker. "Have you ever been sitting at your desk shuffling papers, when you got a nasty paper cut?" I asked. Playing the part of the office worker, seated at my desk, he nodded while taking copious notes. "Or have you ever pulled open your desk drawer and banged your knee?" I continued. "Wouldn't it be great," I concluded, "to have a first aid kit handy in your drawer?" "This is great stuff," he said, writing furiously.

I looked at my watch and noticed that an hour had passed. I had to leave in half an hour for an appointment, and I needed the time to pull a few things together. "Look," I said, "I really need to get back to work." The man rose, thanking me profusely for my time and help. As he was leaving he laughed and said, "For the first time I think I may have some idea of what I'm doing!"

About 40 minutes later, I locked the door to my office and headed to the lobby to let the receptionist know I was leaving. As I approached her desk, I noticed a first aid kit sitting on the corner of her desk. "Tammy," I said, "I see you have a first aid kit on your desk." "Yeah," she said. "I just bought it." Before I could comment she asked, "Have you ever been shuffling papers at your desk and got a bad paper cut?" I grinned as I walked out to my car. "Now there's a guy," I thought, " who's going to go far."

Throughout our careers, most of us are exposed to more than a few learning opportunities—seminars, workshops, and training programs. Many people attend these sessions with the best of intentions. Some even have a genuine enthusiasm for the process. When the program is concluded, they leave with the intention of doing better. When they return to the office, they even make a special file to hold their handouts. The materials are placed in the folder, and the folder is put in the filing cabinet. And learning comes to a screeching halt.

One of the great questions of life must be: What do we do with all the knowledge we acquire? If that knowledge is relegated to the bottom drawer of a filing cabinet (literally or figuratively), the chances of it making a difference are seriously compromised. Instead of filing new knowledge away for future use, we need to look for the earliest opportunity to apply it. Life does have a way of revealing its most profound secrets in the simplest of ways, but only to those who, like the man who burst into my office, are willing to learn from it.

Turning failure into victory

1. Recognize that you do not have all the answers. It's a tough thing to admit sometimes, especially in a world that often sees that as a shortcoming.

2. Be willing to ask for help. The thing I liked most about the man in my office—the thing that made me give him an hour of my time—was his humility. It was more important to him to have the answers than it was to give the appearance of knowing it all already. Being willing to ask for direction, while not always easy, is essential for growth.

3. This is the most important step, one I call the Law of Utilization. Be willing to apply in reality what you learn in theory. Make a commitment to try to apply in the real world something you've learned in class.

Conclusion

According to the National Pest Management Association, the cost of damage throughout North America caused by termites exceeds that caused by fires, storms, and floods combined. The cost of these little buggers in New Orleans alone tops $300 million each year. What's true in nature is also true in business: Little things can have big consequences.

When *Management Mess-Ups* came out in a Chinese language edition, I wondered what the interest would be. As it turns out, considerable. I soon learned that business leaders in China are hungry for information on American-style management. While the rest of the world worries about the global impact of outsourcing, China is focusing on reducing costs and increasing productivity through good management practices. In other words, they're paying close attention to the "termites."

Companies looking for a sustainable competitive advantage may want to consider a "back to basics" strategy in management as well. By identifying the pitfalls to avoid—and then doing so—managers will not only give their companies a competitive edge, they'll give valued employees an incentive to hang around. As one person told me, "Even if you work for an average company, if you have a good boss, you have a great job."

Good luck finding (and eliminating) the "termites!"

Index

About the Author

Mark Eppler is a professional speaker and seminar leader specializing in leadership, management, and customer service issues. His client list covers a broad range of industries and includes such notables as GE, Procter & Gamble, 3M, Cintas, Scripps Howard, Tyco Healthcare, and the IRS, to name a few. Mark's humorous and engaging style has made him a popular speaker at meetings and conferences worldwide.

Mark is a graduate of Indiana University, where he also served as an adjunct lecturer in business and management. He is a recipient of the University's prestigious *Robert Richey Award for Teaching Excellence*. In addition, he has more than 20 years at the executive level in the electronics industry, most recently as president and COO of a component manufacturer.

Mark is the author of the best selling book, *Management Mess-Ups: 57 Pitfalls You Can Avoid (And Stories of Those Who Didn't)*. In 2000, Kinkos selected *Management Mess-Ups* as one of eight business books to be carried in its copy centers nationwide. A popular seller, the book has been "in stock" ever since. Now available in a Chinese language edition, Mess-Ups has been featured on such media sources as ABCNEWS.com, *USA Today*, NBC-TV, and Investors Business Daily, to name a few.

Mark's second book, *The Wright Way: 7 Problem-Solving Principles From The Wright Brothers That Can Make Your Business Soar*, has been described by the AMA as a "perfect blend of savvy business guidance and historical adventure story." The book was voted one of the top 10 business books in 2004 by the *Globe and Mail*, Canada's largest newspaper. The book is also available in a Korean language edition.

For more information on Mark Eppler, or the speeches and seminars he presents, please contact:

MARK EPPLER & Associates
126 Lakefield Drive
Milford, OH 45150-1884 USA
Phone/Fax: 513-576-9746
Cell phone: 513-608-4680
E-Mail: mark@markeppler.com